MIDDLE SCHOOL CASE STUDIES

Challenges, Perceptions, and Practices

Charles R. Watson
James Madison University

Merrill,
an imprint of Prentice Hall
Upper Saddle River, New Jersey   *Columbus, Ohio*

Library of Congress Cataloging-in-Publication Data
Watson, Charles R. (Charles Ray)
      Middle school case studies : challenges, perceptions, and practices/
Charles R. Watson.
         p.   cm.
      Includes bibliographical references and index.
      ISBN 0-13-197922-1
      1. Middle schools—United States—Case studies. 2. Middle school
teachers—United States—Case studies. 3. Middle school students—United States—
Case studies.   I. Title.
   LB1623.5.W38   1997
   373.2'36'0973—dc20   96-11923
                                                        CIP

Cover art: Paul Klee/SuperStock
Editor: Debra A. Stollenwerk
Production Editor: Mary M. Irvin
Design Coordinator: Julia Zonneveld Van Hook
Text Designer: Mia Saunders
Cover Designer: Brian Deep
Production Manager: Laura Messerly
Electronic Text Management: Marilyn Wilson Phelps, Matthew Williams, Karen L.
    Bretz, Tracey Ward

This book was set in Dutch 823 by Prentice-Hall, Inc. and was printed and bound
by Quebecor Printing/Book Press. The cover was printed by Phoenix Color Corp.

Printed in the United States of America

10 9 8 7 6 5 4 3 2 1

ISBN: 0-13-197922-1

Prentice-Hall International (UK) Limited, *London*
Prentice-Hall of Australia Pty. Limited, *Sydney*
Prentice-Hall of Canada, Inc., *Toronto*
Prentice-Hall Hispanoamericana, S. A., *Mexico*
Prentice-Hall of India Private Limited, *New Delhi*
Prentice-Hall of Japan, Inc., *Tokyo*
Simon & Schuster Asia Pte. Ltd., *Singapore*
Editora Prentice-Hall do Brasil, Ltda., *Rio de Janeiro*

PREFACE

My reasons for writing this casebook grew from my experience as a middle grades teacher for many years as well as from my present position as an educator of other middle grades teachers. During both periods of my life, I have been struck by two things, one negative, one positive. First, I am tired of hearing how difficult and problematic middle school students can be and of seeing how the various mass media support and encourage this perception. Second, I am amazed at the efforts of energetic, knowledgeable, committed, and dedicated middle school professionals in educating these wonderful students. Teachers, principals, counselors, custodians, cooks, support staff, and others take what we call the "middle school philosophy" and all its complex elements, and use it to build successful, responsive schools for young adolescents. These activities often take place quietly and efficiently in the face of complex and sometimes faddish reform efforts.

Since the early 1960s the movement to transform junior high schools into responsive, caring, and effective learning environments for students has grown and been sustained by successes, challenges, and the work of numerous middle school professionals, at both the school and university levels. However, even as the movement has grown, the complexities of the educational environment have made the job of transforming middle school education even more difficult. The social mores of American culture have changed dramatically, and the changes have had enormous effects on all levels of schooling.

This book is written with the practicing professional in mind, as well as those who will soon be practicing professionals; indeed, the teachers who will usher in the twenty-first century will undoubtedly see even more cultural and societal shifts. The complex road to effective teaching of middle school students can be negotiated in spite of the enormous social and

political challenges facing teachers, administrators, and parents. The challenge of finding the way is a perplexing one for both experienced and inexperienced school professionals. This book is intended as a way for middle
school educators and parents to examine many of the issues, problems,
and perceptions in a format that injects some reality into a study of middle
school constructs and contexts.

The Middle School Philosophy

The phenomenon known as the "middle school philosophy" is unique in its
depth and level of educational change. This "philosophy" is actually less a
philosophy than a set of structures and practices that allow teachers and
administrators to synergistically combine these practices into a school culture that recognizes the uniqueness of the middle school age group. It
allows for teachers, principals, and parents to become committed teams of
instructional and curricular experts, teams that may bring about increased
levels of educational achievement and student success.

A major foundation element for these practices is a way of thinking—
about students, about learning, about teaching, and about how the culture
of schools should reflect this. The "middle school philosophy," therefore, is
a great many things, none easily defined or easily put in place.

The uniqueness of this set of practices poses exceptionally difficult
challenges. This reform and restructuring movement contains elements of
both first-order and second-order change;* that is, the middle school
movement involves changes that fundamentally alter the structure of
schooling as well as those that build upon or improve existing practices.

To change from a departmentally structured junior high school to an
interdisciplinary team-based middle school is complex and difficult—so
much so that the rate of success speaks highly for the thousands of dedicated middle school professionals. Yet the process remains fraught with
challenges and difficulties, which are often exacerbated by the increasingly
problematic culture within which these changes take place. This book is
designed with those challenges in mind.

The challenges posed in this book should not be viewed as either
unsolvable or typical. Many teams in middle schools operate effectively
and in the best interests of children; many principals and dynamic leaders
in middle schools consistently forge ahead, leading and improving their
schools; many schools have curricula and materials that are rich, genera-
tive, relevant, interesting, and important; many supportive parents and

---

*Cuban, L. (1985). A fundamental puzzle of school reform. *Phi Delta Kappan, 69* (5), 340–344.

community partners enter into strong, positive partnerships with teachers, teams, and schools; many teachers go about the business of middle school teaching with freshness, creativity, energy, knowledge, and love; and, of course, thousands of wonderful and diverse middle school students continue to challenge us to do what is morally correct, pedagogically sound, and in the best interests of American culture.

Book Organization

This casebook is organized around the central themes and structures that drive middle schools. Chapter 1 presents some of the challenges that teachers face every day when dealing with **middle school students.** More growth and change occur in children at this time in their lives than in any other period except the neonatal period and infancy. The challenges surrounding knowledge of middle school students are therefore critical to understanding the philosophy that drives the process. Teachers and administrators must hold tacit and meaningful understandings that reach beyond teaching strategies and middle school structures. They must have a profound and empathetic sense of how middle school students think, learn, feel, and behave; in turn, these understandings must be supported and nourished by a love of middle school students. Good middle school teachers love what they do, and this is because they love the students in their charge.

Chapter 2 is focused on another critical element of middle schools: **teachers and interdisciplinary teaching teams.** Middle school teachers, no longer isolated in their profession, are faced with new ways to relate to students and also to their peers. The pressures placed on teachers in interdisciplinary teams are new, exciting, and often fraught with human frailties. Interdisciplinary teams often force teachers to be more vulnerable, more open to scrutiny, and more accountable, and to act in a more professional manner. Teaming requires communication and collaboration in a way that has historically been absent from the profession. Teams require teachers to publicly demonstrate their knowledge of content and pedagogy; teams also often compel teachers to defend their teaching actions, choice of strategy, selection of content, and personal educational philosophy.

Chapter 3 focuses on the **middle school curriculum.** The cases presented do not offer new suggestions for the content of the curriculum, but they do suggest that new approaches toward integration of subject matter are rewarding and effective, though difficult. Curriculum integration can also take on different meanings, forms, strategies, and levels of richness. However, regardless of the form or meaning, any approach must connect students with content in a relevant, meaningful manner. The competition for students' attention and intellectual curiosity is fierce, and the competitors—television, video games, and computer simulations, for instance—are very good at grabbing their attention.

Chapter 4 presents cases in the area of **instruction**—the vehicle and mechanism by which teachers connect content with students' minds, intellects, and curiosities. It is also perhaps the most difficult area in which to bring about change, because it involves altering or disposing of long-standing practices through which many teachers have perceived themselves as personally and professionally successful. Yet today's students are different from earlier generations, and many of the old ways do not work for these students; middle school students are probably much more "street smart" than their teachers and are certainly more likely to challenge their teachers. Instruction must change to meet the challenges these students present. Once again ferocious media competition, especially television, gets better and better at instructing students. This chapter concerns some of the actual instructional techniques that are associated with middle schools, as well as the intellectual and emotional challenges faced by teachers as they attempt to fundamentally alter their actions and thinking.

Chapter 5, on **middle school administration,** looks at several common situations faced by administrators. As principals attempt to lead faculties through the difficult process of change, they may find themselves mired in sticky and complex human fears and professional disagreements. Teachers can become deeply resistant to changing practices and habits, especially if the changes run counter to their past experiences. Principals and change agents must carefully examine this phenomenon of resistance, because teacher resistance can easily be used as an excuse to disguise implementation problems.* Parents are also becoming increasingly vocal and involved in schools, and although this involvement is important and desirable, it also complicates the situation and creates a need for new and more effective ways to communicate ideas and concepts. The challenges presented in chapter 5 are increasingly common in all levels of public and private education; fortunately, they are problems that have solutions.

The cases presented in chapter 6 describe challenges and problems that face teachers and principals who are committed to developing **exploratory and prevocational programs** for middle school students. These programs are often perceived as unimportant by political figures and legislators, so they become easy targets for fiscal and budget reductions. They are, however, a crucial ingredient for many other middle school programs; they are also extremely powerful and important parts of the responsive curriculum. Exploratory, intramural, and prevocational approaches add yet another level of complexity to daily schedules, work loads, staffing pat-

*Fullan, M. (1991). *The new meaning of educational change.* New York: Teachers College Press.

terns, and instructional change. It is not uncommon for teachers involved in exploratory or intramural programs to take on additional obligations, adding to their already heavy loads.

Chapter 7 examines a fundamental aspect of middle school education: **leadership.** The leadership teams and teacher leaders described in this chapter call to mind a parallel to administration, and indeed teacher leaders often take action and make decisions in areas that once fell more directly into the principal's responsibility. Site-based governance and management in middle schools often rely on teams of teacher leaders who are in a better position to experience problems and solutions. In this way the resolution of problems can occur at the level most appropriately responsible for implementing solutions. Most important, however, are the more democratic decision-making processes regarding students and the development of responsive practices; if the culture of a middle school is to reflect responsiveness to its students, decisions reached by groups of teacher leaders will be much more effective than decisions by fiat. The challenges facing teacher leaders, however, are intricate and often perplexing, particularly when most teachers have had little or no training or education with respect to making these kinds of decisions and no experience working in such environments.

Parents and community involvement are topics covered in chapter 8. As the spotlights of public, political, and media scrutiny shine on schools, parents and parent involvement become increasingly important. Parents and parent groups traditionally have had little more than advisory or supportive roles in schools. Good middle schools, however, work diligently to involve parents and community groups in meaningful and important ways. Groups external to the school—businesses, industries, social agencies, churches, and other public and private groups—are viewing their involvement in schools not only as a benefit but as a moral imperative. Schools, especially those experiencing budgetary or financial constraints, often see this involvement as a two-edged sword, providing needed resources while cutting into the control and management of the schools. Teachers and principals, as educational reformers and leaders of innovation, are therefore faced with yet another complicating factor in their path toward responsive education, as these groups become more knowledgeable and educationally sophisticated. The problems presented in this chapter may not be as common as others in the book, but middle school leaders must be ready to prepare for and meet these challenges.

Chapter 9, a chapter devoted to **middle school athletics,** may come as a surprise to many readers, but athletics can be one of the most contentious areas as middle schools move toward practices more appropriate for students. American culture places great importance on competition and winning. Although sports and athletics are an appropriate and enjoyable way of addressing the culture's need for competition, traditional athletic programs can have detrimental and even destructive effects on middle school students. During this developmental period, children's bodies are growing at a rapid and varying pace, and the potential for injury is more pronounced, especially in contact sports. A quick look down the sideline at a junior high or middle school football game will reveal considerable variance in physical size and development. During this period of development, children are keenly aware of their athletic shortcomings, their clumsiness, and their developing bodies; associated with this awareness are negative emotional responses, doubts, and wide swings in self-esteem and self-concept. Even the best middle schools are often caught in the dilemma of providing interscholastic sports and athletics at the risk of physical and emotional injury, as students, parents, and communities pressure schools for competitive sports and athletics. School communities garner a measure of their identity and self-respect from their sports teams, and the demand for athletics and competitive sports often reflects students' need for a measure of school success, particularly if academic success might be less likely. The challenges faced by the teachers and coaches in the cases presented in this chapter are far from uncommon.

Finally, chapter 10 presents situations, cases, and problems that point to **the future.** American culture is becoming less and less homogeneous, and school populations and problems often mirror that diversity. Schools also reflect social and cultural problems; they are indeed microcosms of the larger society. Few, if any, schools are not concerned with violence, teen pregnancy, racism and hatred, diminishing literacy and skills development, sexuality, sexual behavior, firearms and other weapons, and other social ills. Middle schools are not immune to these societal ills, and middle school students are perhaps most vulnerable to these contagions as they begin to try to make sense of the world. Teachers are faced with challenges that no preparatory program can possibly address; they must meet and overcome these challenges each day of their professional lives, and they often succeed in spite of diminishing resources and support. The situations described in the chapter represent only a few of the challenges that nearly all teachers must face as the third millennium approaches.

The Case Study Approach

The use of case studies and vignette analyses in education has a rich history, surpassed only by the history of case analysis in cultural ethnography and business. Educators are finding that case studies help teachers and change agents prepare for problems that are commonly found during the change process. Cases are also used to prepare novice and preservice teachers for the realities of life in school. Carter (1993)* suggested convincingly that "the analysis of story is of central importance to the field of education." Thorough, knowledgeable, and public case analyses can help communities match potential solutions with cultural and educational values and goals.

Case studies also provide a natural method for collaborative discussion and problem defining and solving. Good middle schools operate with effective teams and a collaborative spirit; effective and realistic case studies, used either in school settings or university settings can become models of team problem solving or be used as a focal point for simulating team settings.

Using the Book

There are several ways to use this book. No matter how it is used, the reader and user must remember that no case or context is ever identical to another. Indeed, the same events in schools can be described differently by different participants. Cases should be viewed as slices of school life that can be observed, examined, dissected, analyzed, and discussed. The identifying details of the events or situations depicted in this book are all fictitious, yet many readers will quickly identify with the situations and school contexts. It is important to recognize, however, that cases such as these can rarely be analyzed in the same manner or to the same extent as a case in accounting, for example. Human beings are at work in schools, working on and with other human beings; the complexity is enormous and powerful. We each bring to case analysis our own experience, education, personality, learning style, background, philosophy, and imagination. Kowalski, Weaver, and Henson (1994)* suggest that case readers filter situational knowledge through a set of personal beliefs and knowledge, causing multiple interpretations of judgments. The cases therefore have no clear, right-or-wrong solutions—just multiple ones, some better than others.

Readers of the cases will also note that elements of middle school themes, structures, and organizations wind throughout each topical area; interdisciplinary teams, in particular, are central to middle school practices and are found in nearly every area. This emphasis allows the book to

---

*Carter, K. (1993). The place of story in the study of teaching and teacher education. *Educational researcher, 22* (1), 5–12.

*Kowalski, T. J., Weaver, R. A., & Henson, K. T. (1994). *Case studies of beginning teachers.* New York: Longman.

be used to focus on more than one aspect of middle school practices without marring the contextual integrity of an individual case.

One method of using this casebook is to examine an area of middle school practice or structure using the cases as an advance organizer. The cases can serve as a framework around which discussion of the topics takes place. Exploration of the various facets of the cases will help readers understand the realities of middle school practice as they pertain to a given topic.

Another method is to have small groups of teachers or students read the cases individually, identify the central aspects of the cases, discuss the points presented at the end of each case, and then present their findings to a larger group. This method is particularly useful when a staff, faculty, or class are examining specific areas of practice.

Following any case discussion or analysis, the case contexts and central points should be refocused locally. For example, if the casebook is being used primarily as an advance organizer to study a problem area, the discussion leader should carefully place the case challenges or problems into a local context. In this manner, readers will be looking at both the cases and their own situations analytically and thoroughly.

Finally, the cases in the book may be used as culminating discussion activities for groups studying middle school concepts, practices, and structures. Schools, school districts, teacher educators, and education students often examine middle school practices as presented by experts, theorists, and writers, and these examinations are important facets of learning about middle schools. However, it is equally important that those who study middle school education experience, at least vicariously, the realities associated with implementing these practices. As mentioned earlier, combining innovative practice with changes to existing structures and practices is a difficult and complex task. It is hoped that readers of the book will use the cases constructively as they continue to develop middle schools that are responsive and effective.

Acknowledgments

Over the past twenty years, many people have furnished information for this book. Some of the cases are ones that I lived, some are those that I witnessed, and some are those that have been told to me. To these wonderful storytellers and teachers, I am sincerely and deeply grateful. To the hundreds of remarkable middle school students who put up with me as I struggled with new ideas, new content, new methods, and new customs and cultures, I am profoundly thankful. I also appreciate greatly the thoughtful comments and suggestions of the reviewers of my manuscript:

Jeannette Abi-Nader, Gonzaga University; George Belden, North Georgia College; Charles M. Carter, Barton College; Thomas O. Erb, University of Kansas; Judith L. Irvin, Florida State University; Marie Paula Hardy, Spalding University; Ann Lockledge, University of North Carolina at Wilmington; and Dennis Pataniczek, State University of New York at Brockport.

Several friends and colleagues provided valuable insights and assistance as this book grew from a few cases used in a course to its present form. My mentor, Allan Glatthorn, of East Carolina University, examined early versions of the cases and gave helpful and constructive advice. Teresa Harris helped me look at case studies as stories. Gerry Green was patient with me as I tested new cases and ideas on students. Jerry Benson, my dean, encouraged me throughout the process. Finally, my friend and colleague Deborah Quigley encouraged me and gave me her wisdom about teaching, learning, schools, and children; she also devoted much of her valuable time to reading the drafts of the cases.

To these and all others whose lives revolve around children, teaching, and learning, I give my thanks.

CONTENTS

1

STUDENTS

The Case of the Strong Leader
The Case of the Bad Hair Days
The Case of the New Teacher
The Case of the Spreading Problems
The Case of the No-hat Rule

DURING THE YEARS of pre- and early adolescence, the human body changes more than at any other time except during the neonatal period and infancy. These changes envelop the entire range of human development—intellectual, emotional, social, physical, and moral. In no case do two human beings develop at the same rate or time, but this variability in the developmental stage should not be taken as a denial of commonalities. Dorman, Lipsitz, and Verner (1985) suggest that as a school group, early adolescents have several needs:

- a diverse approach to teaching, curriculum, and scheduling
- self-exploration and self-definition
- meaningful participation in school and community
- positive social interaction with peers and adults
- physical activity

1

- competence and achievement
- structure and clear limits

Intellectually, middle school students are curious about the world, yet they see it through in a very concrete way. Most remain at the stage of concrete operations throughout the middle school years (Esom & Wolmsley, 1980). They are, however, stretching themselves intellectually as they become more aware of the complex and often counterintuitive knowledge presented to them in most middle level content. The student who has no difficulty understanding a complex algebraic equation may have great difficulty comprehending the difference between a county, a state, and a nation. Many also have difficulty with the concept of extended periods of time, particularly as expressed in historical terms. The concept of millennia may be understood on the same terms as decades or centuries (numbers of years), but with little understanding of the scope of past time. The idea that humans lived during the same period as the dinosaurs, though incorrect, can be a very concrete one for middle school students.

The psychosocial characteristics of middle school students can baffle not only students themselves but also their teachers and parents. The transition to middle school nearly always brings about lower self-esteem (Cotton, 1985), and self-esteem can swing easily as students struggle with media messages, the need for peer approval, the need for family and parental support, and the need for positive relationships with teachers and other adults (George & Alexander, 1993). Interaction, communication, and other social skills are critical needs for students (Hall, 1987), yet these areas often appear to receive less emphasis in middle schools as subject matter and content become more complex, demanding, and time-consuming. The social and behavioral pressure exerted by peers, although very strong and influential, is only one consideration for early adolescents' decisions. Scheidlinger (1984) suggested that peer group influence is generally not responsible for negative behavior, but that it can be influential as a mechanism for reflecting a child's ideas or potential behaviors. Middle school students' reactions and conformance to peer group values tend to drive their behaviors toward a common set of norms. With respect to school, in most cases middle schoolers view school first as a place to meet with their friends and peers. The pressures related to their social groups can often be fierce and imposing, but many of the friendships formed during the middle school years are likely to last through adulthood.

During the middle school years, students are forming a sense of personal identity that may still feel fleeting and uncertain. They are bombarded with messages from peers, adults, and the media, and without guidance and acceptance from adults, they find it difficult to make choices about identity and values. Feldman and Elliott (1990) suggest that this period of life is pivotal, especially with respect to how society views the early adolescent—as neither adult nor child.

Schools designed to accommodate these variations of development often face unique challenges. Teachers must use a variety of instructional strategies, they must be keenly aware of the students' rapid changes, and they must be attuned to ways to alter not only instruction but the environments within which they work. The teachers who provide the instruction and environment must also be ones who enjoy working with this age group and have strong empathetic responses to the students. Good middle school teachers often remember how it was to be a middle school student.

An **interdisciplinary team** can also provide an element of stability and care during these difficult years. A group of teachers who are knowledgeable about the age level and the students' developmental needs can plan and implement strong instructional programs that not only accommodate needs but also help foster social, intellectual, physical, and emotional development.

The following cases are not uncommon ones, but we must remember that each school culture, each teacher, each student, each problem can be quite different, depending on local and community situations and cultures.

The Case of the Strong Leader

The seven girls were all dressed in similar fashion: baggy printed shorts, huge T-shirts, white socks, and mixed colors of tennis shoes. All wore obvious makeup and lipstick, and five of the seven wore their hair in fluffy, long curls. The other two girls had very short hair, stylishly cut. They were all standing together in the seventh-grade Gold Team hall of Midland Middle School. Other students were also standing around the hall, some digging in lockers, others talking, but most were walking toward the classrooms along the hall. The group of girls was listening intently to one of the two short-haired girls. Wisps of conversation floated from the group.

"Gawd, my mother would kill me if I cut my hair," said the girl with the longest hair.

"Well, my mother didn't have a choice. It's my hair, and that's that—I'll do what I want with it."

"I sure wish my mom would . . . Geez, that's the last bell." The conversation was interrupted by the electronic squeal of the "bell" and a noticeable rise in the hall noise level as students slammed locker doors, dropped books, and slowly headed for the classrooms.

Maryann Watson, the seventh-grade team leader and science teacher, watched as the students noisily found their places at the tables. Elizabeth, the girl with the new short haircut, was the last to enter the room and slowly made her way to the seat at the table nearest Ms. Watson's desk.

"Good morning, Elizabeth, great haircut!" Ms. Watson spoke quietly to Elizabeth as she took her seat. Elizabeth appeared to ignore the compliment and rolled her eyes at her tablemates. As she dropped her bookbag on the floor, her response was, "How long do I have to sit with these geeks?"

"You're the geek, bat breath," said Tommy Baker, one of Elizabeth's tablemates, smiling.

"Look people, it's Monday. Let's not start off the week this way, okay? Elizabeth, first of all, I don't appreciate your use of that word, and Tommy, cool it, okay? Can I have everyone's attention? Today we're going to continue our examination of cell structure by comparing animal cells with plant cells. We're going to do that by looking closely at some cells through the microscopes. Okay, you know the drill: equipment managers, get the microscopes out, while I point out the sequence of what we're going to do."

The class proceeded smoothly, as students examined leaf cells and animal cell slides, discussing their findings and making drawings of the cells. However, during the Gold Team meeting later that day, the subject of Elizabeth's behavior was brought up for discussion.

"She called her tablemates a name in my class, but other than that, everything went fairly well for a change. A far cry from last week, when she said she was going to the bathroom and instead met her buddies by the cafeteria telephone. I never did figure out who they were going to call." Maryann spoke quietly in her classroom as she looked at the table where Elizabeth had sat earlier.

"Well, you had her for first period. By the time she and her gang came to my room, they had cooked up a plan to refuse to do any work at all. Said they were 'on strike' until things changed. I just gave them all zeros," Richard Kramer, the English and language arts teacher, said. He was known for his serious attitude and rather inflexible classroom management style. "Sarah came to me after class, though, crying. She said she really didn't want to follow Elizabeth, but she didn't have a choice. I told her if she got the work to me tomorrow, I'd accept it for partial credit."

"Why, Richard, you're turning softie on us!" Marilyn Vance, the social studies teacher, laughed and poked Richard on the shoulder. "They did the same thing to me, except a couple did their work anyway—Sarah and Janie. You know, this thing with Elizabeth has gone about as far as I can put up with it. This is October, and I don't think I can stand this for the rest of the year. And how many times have we talked to her mom? Six? That sure hasn't done any good."

"Seven, if you count the open house," Maxine Harris, the most experienced teacher of the group, said. "I had her last period, in pre-algebra, and you know that only one other of that group is in that class. I took this note away from Elizabeth just as she was about to pass it." Maxine unfolded a sheet of notebook paper and handed it across the table so the others could see it. "I think it's time we did something."

"My God, Max, she says she's going to cut Sarah's and Janie's hair! And according to this, they're going to hold them down to do it! And they are cooking up a plan to get them alone!"

"Hold on, Maryann, do you think she can get the others to do something like this? I know she's the leader, but do you really think she has that kind of power?" Richard leaned forward over the table as he spoke.

"Well, let's see. She talked about twenty-five kids out of going on the skating trip with us, she threatened all the girls out of trying out for cheerleading so she could get a shot at it, and some of the boys are afraid of her, too. Tim Mathews told me that she knew stuff about all of them and would tell on them unless they did what she wanted. Luckily, most of the boys don't care. And, oh, yes, let's not forget the smoking incident. Do you really think she wasn't behind that? Her mom certainly believed her and not us, that's for sure." Maryann stood up and began to walk around the room as she continued. "You know, at first we just blamed peer pressure and the like, but this is getting pretty serious."

"Well, that has to be some of it. Those girls talk alike, dress alike, act alike, and I'm sure they must spend a lot of time talking on the phone in the evenings for them to always come to school looking like clones of each other." Maxine shrugged and went on, "But the thought of her cutting off all of Sarah's beautiful hair just gives me the creeps. All right, who's going to do what?"

Discussion Points

1. Elizabeth is obviously a leader of her peer group, but some of her leadership qualities are taking her friends in the wrong directions. How typical is this? What other problems could arise from this type of leadership?

2. What are some steps that the team might take at this point? List at least two options, and discuss the likelihood of success.

3. What developmental characteristics is Elizabeth exhibiting?

The Case of the Bad Hair Days

The building, formerly a high school, had been built in the early 1950s. Restoration and modernization had transformed it into a fairly workable middle school, but the Bear Team still had to use one of the "permanently temporary" buildings adjacent to the old school. When the eighth-grade Bear students changed from one teacher to another, at least one-fourth of them had to walk between the buildings. Although the distance was relatively short, about thirty yards, the prevailing winds along this area seemed to form a tunnel along the sidewalk where the students walked. From January through May, it was not uncommon for a strong wind, twenty-five to thirty-five miles per hour, to be whipping through the area.

All four of the Bear teachers were experienced professionals. Each had been recognized as exemplary in his or her field, and all had been teachers of the year in the school district. The move to interdisciplinary teams had taken place two years ago, and the Bear Team was considered one of the best in the district.

"Well, do you think we'll have class before noon today?" asked Rick, the Bear Team social studies teacher. "They don't care if we stand here and glare at them, they all head for the bathroom on windy days. Look, there goes Tanya—honor roll student, and all-around great kid—but her hair is more important than social studies today!" He grimaced as he spoke to Beth, the team science teacher.

"Yeah, and the boys aren't much better," she replied. "I don't know, Rick, it's not a capital offense, but some days I feel like screaming when they come trotting into my class five minutes late. And tardy slips sure don't work, either. They don't mind spending a few minutes after school if it means coming to class with every strand of hair in place." Beth turned and started toward her science room, and said over her shoulder, "Go yell into the bathrooms, Rick. It's your turn."

As simple as it appeared, the problem of wind-blown hair was complex and difficult to solve. Almost hourly, the Bear students would rush to the restrooms with combs, brushes, and hairspray in hand and attempt to repair the damage done by the wind. The small restrooms, the extent of hair damage, the small mirrors, and the velocity of the wind all combined to ensure that most of the students who made the restroom dash were late to class—sometimes by as much as three or four minutes.

The team had tried several solutions. At first, they gave tardy slips to each late student; however, the students appeared almost happy to take a tardy slip if they could take the time to fix their hair. Next, the team decided to stop the trips to the restroom between classes and schedule times for restroom breaks before classes started in the morning, around the lunch period, and just before dismissal. Several parents called and complained about this policy, since it appeared that students were complaining to their parents about not being allowed to go to the restroom when there was a physiological need.

The next attempt at a solution was to station the teachers inside the restrooms between classes, especially on windy days. This seemed to work, but the teachers weren't happy about spending so much time in the restrooms between classes. There was very little time between classes—only four minutes—to straighten the room and prepare for the next group. This solution also led to many more requests for bathroom passes during class times, and when the students returned, it was obvious that they had spent time working on their hair.

The Bear teachers were near their wits' end with the situation. "Okay, guys, let's talk about the tardy problem again," Marsha Bryant, the team leader and math teacher, said as she opened the daily team meeting. The two-item agenda was written on the blackboard: tardies and report cards. "We've got to set a time to get together and do report cards, but that won't take too long—what we need to settle is this tardy problem. It was awful today! None of my classes, and I'm sure none of yours, started anywhere near on time. What are we going to do?"

"Heck, I don't know, what haven't we tried yet? I'm out of ideas," responded Rick.

"They just don't seem to care if they're late or not—as long as they get their hair fixed before class," said Sean, the team's language arts teacher. "It's almost as if some kind of hair epidemic has swept through the team. You know, we've got a great group of kids, and I love 'em all, but this year they seem to be more focused on their appearance than ever before—or at least that's the way it seems to me." He got up from the desk, walked to the pencil sharpener, and sharpened a red pencil. "Maybe we're looking at this all wrong. We're defining the problem as a tardy problem—maybe we should look at what's behind all of this."

Discussion Points

1. The problem in this case has several elements. What are they?
2. What options are available to the team?
3. How should the team go about selecting and implementing an option?
4. What other problems or developmental factors are related to this case?

The Case of the New Teacher

Mary Lou Thomas held her breath as the students wandered into her room. It was the first period of the first day of school; it was also Mary Lou's first day as a teacher, and she was extremely nervous. She had decorated her room with science posters, the periodic table of the elements, a few animal posters, a commercially produced set of safety guidelines, a chart describing a cutaway view of a microscope, a star map of the northern skies, and an old *Star Wars* movie poster. She hoped the room looked inviting as she watched the seventh-graders noisily find seats, throw bookbags to the floor, greet each other, tease each other about clothes and hair, and push and shove each other. She also wondered if she was up to this challenge.

The only job offer she had received had come from this middle school, and she had accepted it only after a great deal of soul searching. After all, she had been trained as a high school biology teacher; she had done her student teaching and all of her practicum work in high schools; and her instructional methods classes had all been geared toward high school students. But she had concluded that there couldn't be that much difference between ninth grade and seventh, so she had accepted the position. Just as she was thinking this, she heard Jim Barker, her teammate, yell at some kids in the hall to hurry to class. Jim then stuck his head in Mary Lou's room and said, "Good luck, there, Mary Lou. Have a great first day!" Before she could respond, he was gone, headed toward his room next door. Well, she thought, here goes . . .

"Settle down, students, the bell rang a couple of minutes ago." As the students began to quiet down, she continued, "My name is Ms. Thomas, and I'd like to welcome you to my room and, ah, the High Flyer Team."

She had nearly forgotten to use the team name, a facet of teaching that was also new to her. She was accustomed to working in a department and, even as a student teacher, having a great deal of independence. As she looked around the room, she began to realize that these students were quite a bit different from those with whom she had recently student-taught.

These students were all shapes and sizes. In the front row of her room, two boys who looked more like third-graders than seventh-graders had their heads down and were looking at their books. Beside one of them was a girl who looked more like a teacher than a student; she was tall and very well developed, and seemed to be bored with everything already. Beside her was another girl who, though not as developed, was dressed in clothes that Mary Lou thought would be appropriate for a young professional woman: dark skirt, blouse with a tie, stockings, and sweater. She carried a handbag. She also had what looked like a hickey on her neck. As Mary Lou's gaze swept the room, she realized that there were some students who were quite small, others who were taller than she was, and some who were obviously overweight. One boy sitting in the back of the room looked to be well over 6 feet tall and perhaps weighed 200 pounds.

They were dressed in different fashions as well. At least this aspect of the room was a little familiar. In her high school, there had been three distinct student styles: preppy, designer clothes, neatly pressed, arranged, and matched; what looked like rummage-sale rejects with torn knees, baggy sweatshirts or sweaters, and tennis shoes that were worn through in many places; and "young professional" garb.

With very few exceptions, however, hair seemed important to all the students. All seemed to have their hair styled and arranged in a manner that complemented or supported their clothing fashion statements.

Mary Lou took roll, read the lengthy list of announcements, and began her class. "Science in the seventh grade is general science. Who can tell me what that means?" she asked.

By the end of the day, Mary Lou was exhausted. The students had behaved fairly well, but she was unaccustomed to the level of activity they demonstrated. It seemed that someone was nearly always asking a question—usually permission to go to the bathroom or in some way to move around the room. Mary Lou had intercepted several notes being passed around the room, and although the notes didn't contain anything much, the interruptions had distracted her. Most students, even the girls, seemed to want to sit in every position imaginable except upright at their desks, and every period she gave her little lecture about sitting up straight to pay attention. No class period went by without at least three students forgetting books, pencils, or notebooks, and she noticed that the students' bookbags contained everything except books and supplies. Most of the copies of the letter and Lab Safety Permission Form she had carefully written for students to take home to parents were scattered all over the floor, and she wondered if any of them would make it home. Her tissue box had run out during third period, and there was a roll of toilet tissue now on her desk. She gathered three combs, two hairbrushes, two cans of hairspray, and a bottle of makeup from around the room. She had given a homework assignment—to read the first section in the textbook—and yet she found nine books lying around the room. Although there was a school rule banning gum chewing, she found gum and candy wrappers sprinkled around the room and in the hallway. Student desks were pointed in all directions, and her own chair had somehow found its way to the back of the room.

Mary Lou had planned on having a pop quiz tomorrow to keep the students on their toes and make sure they kept up with the reading, but as she thought about her day, she began to have doubts as to whether a quiz would do much. Her first attempts at explaining the biologic classification system had been met with stares and looks of confusion; indeed, when she asked questions about her mini-lecture, few of the students could answer her.

As she moved her chair back to her desk and continued to contemplate tomorrow's lesson, Mary Lou wondered if she would make it through the year.

Discussion Points

1. What elements of Mary Lou's seventh-grade classroom seem unusual?
2. Identify some of the challenges Mary Lou seems to be facing with her classes.
3. What steps could Mary Lou's teammates take to help her through this transition?
4. How should Mary Lou begin planning for her subject?
5. What procedures might Mary Lou institute to help her classroom organization?

The Case of the Spreading Problems

The oak cabinets that lined the classroom seemed darker than usual with the overhead fluorescent lights off. The seventh-grade Eagle Team met here in Kiesha Morgan's social studies room three times a week. Because the room was situated around the corner from the lockers and restrooms, it was quieter than some other classrooms and seemed more isolated. The decor and ambiance of the room were also conducive to reflection and quiet work; the walls were neatly hung with framed or bordered student work arranged in topical areas. About half of one wall was being used to display student work titled "Poems and Progress—Poetry as History." The remainder of the room appeared to be decorated in a similar manner, with closets, cabinets, and plastic boxes clearly labeled. Overall, the sense of the room was one of order, care, respect for student work, and organization.

The three teachers who sat at a round table near the rear of the room, however, did not seem to exemplify the same orderliness and organization. All looked tired, and their lesson books, wire trays, and bookbags seemed about to burst with paper, pencils, and books. Kiesha Morgan was the Eagle Team leader, and as she started the meeting, she glanced up at the clock.

"Does anyone have any other things to put on today's agenda?" Kiesha turned and looked at the blackboard as she spoke. Three items were written on the board: basketball game attendance, student behavior, and report cards.

"Well, I'd like to talk about the problems I'm having with my third-period bunch," replied Janelle Jackson, the team's math teacher. She continued, "I don't know what I am doing wrong, but I can't get them to come in, sit down, and get going in less than ten minutes. I don't have that problem with any other period—just third. I think it's the long walk back from the gym that's making them crazy, but I'd like to get some ideas—if not today, then maybe Wednesday."

"I need some time to talk about what Robbie Martin's mother told me on the phone last night," added Richard Becker, the Eagle Team language arts teacher. "She's having a lot of the same problems we are. But we may need a few minutes for this. We need to set up some time to meet with her, too. I hate to see such nice people going through such painful times."

"Okay, so this meeting may take a little longer than I thought. Let's limit ourselves to six minutes a topic as we've been doing—that really seems to help keep us on time," Kiesha said, writing the additional agenda items on the board. "I'll start with the announcements, and then we can talk about the important things."

The announcements took a minute or two, then Kiesha said, "Let's start with behavior. This may also get us to Richard's problems with Robbie and Janelle's third-period class. Let's list the things that are going on that aren't up to our usual standards," she said as she rose and went to the blackboard.

"They are driving me crazy," Janelle said emphatically. Her voice rose as she continued, "They aren't listening to anything I say. I have to tell them what to do and give directions three or four times before half of them even get started on the work. Their grades are slipping, and even when I take points off for being late to class, they keep coming in late. They spend so much time writing notes, looking in the mirror, talking to friends, and worrying about everything *except* school that I can't seem to get through to them. I say we crack down on them and put some real teeth into our discipline plan—more detentions, longer detentions, and lots of in-school suspension."

"I don't know, that sure isn't working with Robbie," said Richard. "His mother has taken away just about every privilege he has, grounded him for the next month, and he is still talking back to her and being disrespectful most of the time. He's being pretty mean and hateful to his sisters, too. From what Ms. Martin tells me, he is really being rebellious at home, and that's a lot of what we are seeing here, too."

"Well, it's not just him," Janelle declared. "I think they are all going crazy. They are so full of hormones and sugar that we can't do anything." She looked up at the walls of the room, paused a moment, and then asked, "Kiesha, how do you get the kids to do such wonderful work? What kind of bribe do you use? And how do you get them to begin working so promptly? Yesterday they were in here and working before it was even time to get started! Our discipline plan calls for three chances: a warning, a student notice, then a parent notice. I am spending a lot of time writing notices and calling parents, and that's no fun. What's your secret?"

Before Kiesha could respond, the door to the room opened and the fourth member of the team, science teacher Vincent Merlino, came rushing into the room, grabbed a chair, pulled it to the table, sat down heavily, and dropped his plan book and two textbooks on the floor beside the chair. He smiled, and in an apologetic tone said, "I'm sorry, folks, but it seems that the district office is going to go ahead and implement the new science curriculum. Susan Rashad just told me that there will even be exit testing at each grade level for the objectives. Kind of scary, you know? Especially when nearly half our kids can't read anywhere near grade level . . . " His voice dropped as he slumped in his chair.

"Hang in there, Vincent, you'll get through this," replied Kiesha. She continued, "We're just talking about the kids' behavior and what we can do to get them into the rooms and working more quickly and quietly. I've noticed that you don't seem to have much of a problem in that area, Vince. Any ideas for us?"

"My goodness, guys, we've got the best group of kids we've had in years. The only problem I've had recently is with Robbie, and even he has calmed down. What kind of problems are you having? Isn't the plan working? I'd hate to see any of our kids in detention or in-school suspension; I'm convinced that all those things do is make things worse. They take a good kid and turn him into a real behavior problem."

Discussion Points

1. This case seems to involve several issues, especially with respect to the students' behavior. What do the teachers' differing perceptions of the problem tell about how the problem should be defined?

2. Most team and school rules are variations on common themes: respect for others and their property, and attention to the work of school. Why would one or more members of the Eagle Team have different levels of behavioral difficulties, when the team's three-step discipline plan seems so clearly defined?

3. One student in particular seems to be causing the team some difficulties. What additional information might the team members gather to help this student?

4. What classroom environmental factors might contribute to the behavior problems the team is facing?

The Case of the No-hat Rule

Although nearly ten years old, Posey Middle School still looked new. Located near the edge of a small midwestern town, the school sat atop a low hill with freshly mowed grass sloping downward from the front of the building to the winding driveway that curved up the hill to the parking lot near the west side of the building. The flatter athletic and physical education fields were along the east side of the building and wrapped around to the center of the rear of the building.

Inside the building, the halls were quiet, as halls often are at the beginning of the school year. A few students walked softly along the polished floors, moving in and out of classrooms. The intersection of two halls was clearly identified by the colors of the walls: one hall was painted a bright sky blue, the intersecting hall was painted a soft, cheerful yellow. The blue hallway was lined with posters and signs that welcomed the Hawk Team students to the team area; a look down the yellow hall quickly identified the Beaver Team area, with posters showing a buck-toothed cartoon beaver holding a Posey Middle School pennant.

An Asian American teacher stood at the doorway of one of the Hawk hall classrooms, and the boy who approached the door appeared to be at least a foot taller than the teacher. As the student moved past her into the room, the teacher reached up, grabbed the bill of his baseball cap, handed it to him, and said, "No hats, Gerald, remember?"

The student continued into the room, grumbling, "Ms. Smith don't care
. . . " His voice tapered off as he went toward his seat across the room.

"That's okay, Gerald, but the rule is 'no hats,' and I like to keep to the
rules. If I catch you wearing it again, I'll have to write you up," Ms. Lee
responded loudly. She looked once more down the hall, then closed the
door and went to her desk.

In a similar classroom on the Beaver hall, Marilyn Ramirez looked at
her watch and said, "Okay, yesterday we were talking about the need for
order and organization for us to learn better. We talked about rules and
rights, and the need for mutual respect. We went over the rules, including
all the ones in the school handbook, and we talked about fights and what
happens to anybody who fights here at Posey. Does anybody have any questions?" She looked around the room, thinking that she would be bored,
too, with all this talk about rules. Kids have talked about rules on the first
day of school every year of their school lives, and it seemed to Marilyn that
it was a waste of time, especially since the kids needed to be reminded constantly. A hand was raised near the back of the room, and Marilyn quickly
and discreetly checked her room list to make sure she had the boy's name
correct. "Jamie, do you have a question?"

"Well, sort of, Ms. Ramirez," Jamie responded with a slight but noticeable Spanish accent. "I don't get the rule about hats."

"What do you mean, Jamie? It's pretty clear. Hats are not to be worn
indoors here at school. It's a school rule that everyone follows."

"Well, I don't get it. Yesterday you told us that the rules were made to
protect people's rights, to keep order, and, you know, make it easy for us to
learn and everything. What's wearing a hat got to do with any of those
things?" Marilyn realized that the question was a good one and that Jamie
wasn't trying to be funny or smart-alecky. The look on his face was one of
serious thoughtfulness.

"Yeah, Ms. R., wearing a hat makes stuff stay in my head," wisecracked
another student seated near Jamie. Jamie looked at the other boy and
frowned, seeming annoyed that his friend wasn't taking the question seriously. A couple of students laughed, and a few began to talk softly.

"I mean it, Ms. Ramirez," responded Jamie, a little louder. "I understand the need for most of the rules we got here, and outside here, too, but
I don't get it about hats. Everybody wears hats, you know, like with teams
and stuff on them. The only people that ever get to wear a hat in this building are the guys on the baseball team, and that's only on game days and
only in the spring during baseball. What's wrong with wearing a hat?"
Jamie was sprawled at his desk, feet splayed out in front of him, his arms
resting on the desktop.

"I understand, Jamie, and I'm taking the question seriously," answered
Marilyn. "It's just that I don't know if I have a good answer. It has been a
rule ever since I came here, and that was when you guys were in kinder-

garten! I think it has to do with manners and respect. It's considered disrespectful to wear hats in a building, and it's bad manners to leave it on when you enter. There was a time when men were supposed to tip their hats to a woman when they passed her on the street. But I've got to be honest with you, Jamie, I can't seem to think of anything else. How about if I try to get you an answer before fifth period? You're in my fifth-period class, aren't you?"

"Yeah, I am. That's cool," Jamie responded.

The Beaver Team had its planning meeting during third period, and Marilyn brought up the subject of the hat rule.

"I don't know, Marilyn," said Rachel Wertheim, "I think there used to be some religious significance to wearing hats in a building, but I can't remember. I remember that we could wear hats when I went to school, but that was in New York City."

"It's simply good manners," said Monica Bailey, the team's most experienced teacher. "Wearing a hat in the house was a big 'no-no' with my Mom and Dad. I remember once my Dad threw my brother's hat in the furnace for wearing it in the house."

"Well, I'm real tired of bugging the kids about hats. I would probably wear one, too, if they'd let me," laughed Tom Stewart, the team's least experienced teacher and the one newest to the school. "Hats are a big deal with kids. As a matter of fact, everybody likes to identify with favorite teams, sports players, and the like. Monica, you even wear that 'Frugal Gourmet' apron when you do science projects." There was a short silence before he continued, "We talk about these kids' need for positive identity, for a way to feel at home, for a way to be comfortable . . . look at these halls! Have you ever seen so many different pictures of beavers? We even have beaver T-shirts. Why not hats?" He looked at his teammates and went on, "I think we should stop enforcing the hat rule. Jamie was right. It doesn't make a lot of sense."

"But these kids need to learn about manners and respect," responded Monica, "and I like the hat rule. I think it's a way to teach the kids respect, and as I said, they sure need a dose of manners. Sometimes I wonder . . . "

Her voice drifted off as Rachel interrupted, "I think I agree with Tom. But if it's a school rule, I don't think we have a choice but to continue to enforce it."

"Well, we could just sort of ignore it," answered Tom.

"But I don't want to ignore it," replied Monica. "I think it's fine. I don't mind the occasional hassle with the kids."

"It's more than occasional, Monica, it happens every day, nearly every period," Rachel said.

"Do all the other teams enforce this rule?" asked Marilyn.

"I don't know, maybe we should see how some of the other teams handle this," said Tom thoughtfully.

Discussion Points

1. How do articles of clothing, such as T-shirts and hats, relate to the developmental characteristics of middle level students?
2. The rule about hats at Posey Middle School has been in effect for a long time. How frequently should rules be reevaluated with respect to need and relevance? How much and what type of input should the students have?
3. The team is in disagreement about the hat rule, but the members seem able to discuss the rule in a collegial manner. How should the team proceed to resolve this conflict?
4. Should team rules and expectations differ from the school's rules? How much leeway should teams and teachers have to interpret and enforce rules? What problems might emerge from this, and how might they be resolved?

References

Cotton, N. (1985). The development of self-esteem and self-esteem regulation. In J. Mack & S. Albon (Eds.), *The development and sustaining of self-esteem in childhood* (pp. 122–150). New York: International Universities Press.

Dorman, G., Lipsitz, J., & Verner, P. (1985). Improving schools for young adolescents. *Educational Leadership, 42* (6), 4–49.

Esom, M. E., & Wolmsky, S. A. (1980). Promoting cognitive and psycholinguistic development. In M. Johnson (Ed.), *Toward adolescence: The middle school years: 79th yearbook of the National Society for the Study of Education, Part 1* (pp. 24–25). Chicago: University of Chicago Press.

Feldman, S., & Elliott, G. (Eds.) (1990). *At the threshold: The developing adolescent.* Cambridge, MA: Harvard University Press.

George, P. S., & Alexander, W. M. (1993). *The exemplary middle School.* Orlando, FL: Harcourt Brace Jovanovich.

Hall, J. A. (1987). Parent-adolescent conflict: An empirical review. *Adolescence, 22,* 767–789.

Scheidlinger, S. (1984). The adolescent peer group revisited: Turbulence or adaptation? *Small Group Behavior, 15,* 387–397.

2

TEACHERS AND TEAMS

The Case of the Uncooperative Teammate
The Case of the Conflicting Team Philosophies
The Case of the Wiped-Out Team
The Case of the Inexperienced Teachers

INTERDISCIPLINARY TEAMS CAN be seen as the cornerstones of good middle schools (Epstein & MacIver, 1990). Designed to be responsive to the needs of the students, good teams share a coherent and consistent basis for instruction, evaluation, and development of educational programs. Through teamwork, teaching professionals link their expertise and experience in such a way that curriculum can become more relevant, interesting, and rigorous. These linkages also provide sound and caring environments for students, within which they are able to experience the affective support that is associated with learning. Teams also provide, in a unique and appropriate way, clear and smooth transition for students between elementary and high school. Interdisciplinary teams of professionals can establish learning environments that are neither the self-contained classrooms of elementary school nor the departmentalized structures of the high school. In this transitional period for the students, the interdisciplinary teams can respond to the unique characteristics of the child who is also experiencing significant and profound personal change.

Optimally, teams have distinct identities that form an instructional and affective "address" for students and teachers. At this "address," the team members share the same students, are often housed in the same area of the building, and share the same schedule. The team identity is more than simply a place or set of team decorations. Teams often develop and share philosophies and teaching strategies that can be used to describe and articulate how the teachers and students feel about school and learning. Teams can be formed in several ways, but most often they consist of two, three, or four teachers (Erb & Doda, 1989).

Team autonomy ensures that the professionals on the team can make decisions with respect to nearly all the educational aspects of students' lives. Teams provide a central point for parental involvement, and often parents become an integral and important part of the team. Team structures also provide operational consistency; rules and operating procedures can be consistent across the team, giving students and teachers a solid sense of stability. Team traditions and ways of recognizing students' achievements provide further solidarity to team structures.

The most important aspect of interdisciplinary teaming is how teachers connect content and curriculum. The interdisciplinary nature of the four core areas—language arts, social studies, mathematics, and science—is known and recognized instinctively, outside of traditional classrooms where they have generally remained separate. Real life is not broken up into distinct subjects or regular time frames.

However, teaming is not easy. As in any human endeavor, complex factors are at play. Teachers' methods and attitudes grow out of teaching experience, education, life experience, and personal philosophy. Personality traits, communication styles, and adult learning modes interact with individual experiences and philosophies and also influence interactions among fellow professionals. Disagreements are not uncommon, yet in the best teams a spirit of compromise, based on what is best for students, is clearly evident. Team leaders attempt to forge cohesion and commitment among the team members. Leadership roles, whether appointed or elected, are difficult and demanding.

✂︎ ✂︎

The Case of the Uncooperative Teammate

Wilson, a school of about 600 students in the sixth, seventh, and eighth grades, was one of two middle schools in the district. The new superintendent was in full support of the school administrators' efforts to implement the "middle school philosophy." In support of Wilson's efforts, the district had paid handsomely for several in-service training sessions for the Wilson staff. The school began its efforts cautiously and had a four-year implementation plan that the staff had enthusiastically endorsed.

Following a particularly good summer workshop, Anna Ross, the principal at Wilson, formed the interdisciplinary teams; the school appeared to be making the transition to this middle school practice very smoothly. The principal was pleased with how the teachers were responding to the new practices and organizations. The teams were meeting daily to discuss students and curriculum, and as a result staff morale was up, student discipline referrals were down, and parent complaints almost nonexistent.

The Starburst Team seemed to be the exception. The team was meeting daily, planning for a more integrated approach to teaching, developing unique ways to recognize students' achievements, discussing students' social and academic progress, and organizing instruction to better address the unique characteristics of the **preadolescent** student—all activities they had learned about over the summer. However, one team member, Janet Wilson, seemed to be having difficulty with this notion of interdisciplinary team teaching.

The sixth-grade Starburst Team had four members. Sue Richards, the language arts teacher and team leader, was an experienced middle school teacher who was often recognized for her innovative teaching strategies and the uncommon success of her students. Her classes were well managed, and her room was extensively decorated with student work and work in progress. Bill Thompson, the science teacher, was also an experienced professional. His room was arranged in a laboratory format, with tables and chairs scattered throughout the room. Jim Michelson was the social studies teacher, and although less experienced than the others, he was using **cooperative learning**, projects, and a differentiated program for his classes, which had **heterogeneous grouping**. Janet was an experienced math teacher, and before teaming began she had enjoyed a great deal of student success, as her students almost always did very well on the year-end tests.

Early in the school year, it became clear that there was a problem with the Starburst Team. The list of problems associated with Janet seemed to grow each week. The trouble began when Janet agreed to simulate a math lesson for parents during the annual back-to-school open house. Ten minutes before her presentation, she complained of a headache, refused to present her lesson, and went home. Instead, Sue and the other teachers presented their daily schedules and went over their programs for the parents.

The next problem occurred when the team decided to allow the students some responsibility and choice during the lunch period. The team decided to simply allow the students to walk quietly to the lunchroom—under their supervision, of course—and to sit in any seat in the lunchroom as long as it was in their designated seating area. The process went beautifully, and the students were pleased to have the opportunity to sit with whom they liked during their short lunch break. However, during one rainy lunchtime, two students argued rather noisily over their preferred seats; Janet, the team teacher on lunch duty that day, unilaterally rescinded the free-seating policy and immediately assigned seats to the students. The other team teachers had no knowledge of what had occurred until the students returned to their classrooms after lunch. After discussing the problem, the team decided to "give the kids another chance" and reinstate the free-seating policy. However, the next time Janet had lunchroom duty, she went back to the assigned seating arrangements, stating that the children had become noisy and rowdy and had lost the privilege of sitting wherever they chose.

The team also had a strict policy of letting team members know when a conversation with a parent took place; indeed, they took great pains to make arrangements to meet with parents as a whole team, and the parents were finding team conferences much more informative and meaningful than those they had experienced in past years. Janet, however, often called parents in for conferences without informing her teammates of the conference or the reason for it. When confronted with this and reminded of the agreement the team had made, she shrugged and stated that the reason for the conference was a "math thing" and there wasn't any reason to involve the team.

The team decided that students were not to eat candy or sweets during the school day; instead, the team kept a supply of oranges, bananas, and other easily stored fruits in their rooms for hungry students. The students appreciated this, and the team felt certain that the program was of great benefit to their classroom efforts; there were few discipline problems, and eating fruit in the room became commonplace and accepted as part of the team's personality. Janet, however, continued to keep a large supply of candy in her room and gave candy to students as a method of rewarding students for good performance on quizzes and tests. She refused the team's offers of fruit and always agreed to stop giving the candy away as soon as it ran out. It didn't seem to run out, and candy in her class became nearly a daily event.

Another problem occurred at the end of the nine-week grading period. The teachers had filled out report cards together, discussing students' progress and problems as they filled in the grade bubbles and wrote comments on the computer sheets. Jim and Bill commented to each other that the process had been informative and seemed to strengthen the team. However, when the printed report cards were distributed, the math grades didn't seem to reflect what had been discussed during the grading session. More than half of Janet's students had failed math, and several top students had received a grade of C or worse. The Starburst students were angry and confused, and the other Starburst teachers were angry and hurt when they realized that Janet had changed her original grades and submitted lower grades and negative comments. Parents called the teachers and the principal complaining about not being told beforehand that there were problems in math. Janet's grade books did indeed reflect the lower grades, and she stated that at first she had intended to be generous and give the students extra points for effort, but had changed her mind at the last moment.

The situation grew worse as the remaining team members began to talk with each other on the telephone in the evenings. It appeared as if Janet always seemed to find a way around, or ignore completely, every policy or program the team agreed to implement. Confrontations were becoming commonplace. The team knew that the students were aware of the problem, because two of the student leaders had complained to Sue about the inconsistencies. Sue had also had several calls from parents complaining about Janet. Whenever she spoke to Janet about the problems, however, Janet dismissed them as something between her and the parents, which shouldn't worry anyone else on the team.

By November, Janet's teammates were barely speaking to her, as she continued to operate as if the team decisions made no difference. In team meetings, she would say very little but would always agree to whatever was being decided; however, she rarely, if ever, followed through on the decisions. Instead, she continued to smile and go about her daily activities as if there were no problems.

Complicating the already complex situation was the remoteness of the principal. Ms. Ross was aware of the problems on the Starburst Team, but refused to take part in solving them. She felt that the team had the responsibility to work things out among themselves, and that she should intervene only in extreme cases. She didn't see this situation as extreme—simply as a case of a teacher needing more time to get used to the idea of interdisciplinary teams.

One day, in a conversation with Sue in her classroom, Bill burst out, "But, Sue, it's not just this stuff about the parents! She agrees to everything and then goes about her business as if we didn't exist. It's affecting the kids, too—have you noticed that we've had to deal with more angry kids in the past few weeks than we have since school started? And they groan when it's time for math. I'm sorry, Sue, but if something isn't done, I'm going to ask for a transfer to either another team or even another school. I really believe we can make this interdisciplinary teaming work, but not when one person can screw things up for us." His red face, waving arms, and pacing around the room added emphasis to his words. "Have you talked with her again?"

"Yes, but she got up and went to the bathroom in the middle of our conversation, and when she came back, all she did was smile and say something about how maybe teaming wasn't her thing, and that she was the best math teacher in the school, and she wouldn't let anything get in the way of her teaching." Sue's head was in her hands as she sat at her desk watching Bill pace. "The more we talked the madder I got and the cooler she got. I finally just left."

"Did you tell Ms. Ross?"

"No, what good would that do? She would tell us the same thing she's told us all year: work it out."

"Maybe if we all sat down with her and tried to explain how we feel . . ."

"I don't know, Bill. I hate to gang up on her that way; she already doesn't feel like much of a team player, and that might make her even worse." Sue's soft voice was full of dread at the thought of such a confrontation. "I hate this team leader business. I'm a teacher, not a leader."

As Bill walked to the door, he said, "Well, we've got to think of something. Let's meet over the vacation and try to work something out. I can't take this any more."

Discussion Points

1. What appear to be the central problems, and whose are they?
2. What are some strategies that might help the team deal with Janet?
3. Who should implement any solutions?
4. How might this type of problem be prevented, and how could preventive measures be implemented?
5. How can this type of problem affect the entire school and its programs?

The Case of the Conflicting Team Philosophies

The interdisciplinary teams at Franklin Middle had been organized and working for three years. The 700-student school was located in a medium-sized district of two high schools, four middle schools, and seven elementary schools. Franklin was the first middle school to implement interdisciplinary teams, and the teams' successes had been instrumental in the district's move toward the "middle school philosophy."

There were four sixth-grade teams, three seventh-grade teams, and three eighth-grade teams. The seventh-grade teams were named the Bears, the Lions, and the Tigers. Over the three-year period, each team had developed its own personality and philosophy; each was different, yet all three appeared to be student-centered in their approaches.

The Lion Team was made up of four teachers, each teaching one of the core disciplines; Mike Lagrange taught language arts, Susan Hoffman taught mathematics, including one section of pre-algebra, Mary Lambert taught social studies, and Lisa Rubin taught the general science classes. All four of the Lion teachers were relatively new to the profession; only Lisa had more than five years' experience. Each of them had graduated from university programs that specialized in middle grades education.

The 110 students on the team were a diverse group, and the team had grouped the students heterogeneously for all subjects, except the twenty-five who were enrolled in pre-algebra. The Lion Team took great pride in the use of cooperative learning, project learning, and differentiated instruction and assignments. The Lion students generally did very well on end-of-course tests, and nearly all of them gained a few percentile points on the year-end achievement tests.

The Lion teachers, however, interpreted the school and district rules more liberally than the Tigers did. The Lion Team classrooms generally had higher noise levels, and students were often found crossing between rooms and going to the library at odd times. The discipline plan called for consistent measures in the event of disruptions or misbehavior, and parents were called often. Few days passed without a parent conference at the end of the schoolday or in the evening. However, very few students were referred to the principal's office for disciplinary action. The teachers dealt with almost all the student problems, and the frequent telephone calls and parent conferences resulted in very positive relationships among the teachers, parents, and students.

The Lion teachers also spent a great deal of time working with students after school and on weekends; the Lion Team leader, Lisa, had requested and received a master key to the building to facilitate the weekend classes and tutoring sessions. The teachers rotated the "Saturday School" duty and often invited parents to attend and work with students. All the teachers appeared to be well liked by students, and the school administrators often used the Lion Team as an example of how teams should deal with discipline problems.

The administrators, however, were less pleased with the noise levels in the rooms and the appearance of the walls of the Lion Team hallway. Students' work was plastered on every available space, and the bulletin boards were all decorated by students. The result was a hallway that often looked tattered and shabby. The administrators who visited and evaluated the teachers noted the hallway and room clutter as well as the general noise level when students changed classes. Both the principal and the district administrators, however, were normally very pleased with the Lion Team, especially since they frequently received letters and calls from Lion parents praising the team. They were willing to accept the extra noise and cluttered hallways and rooms, as long as the parents and students appeared happy.

The Tiger Team also had a diverse group of students, and their test results were even better than the Lions' scores. The team consisted of Mark Cramer, the science teacher and team leader; Karen Black, the social studies teacher; Mildred Rosario, the mathematics teacher; and Judith Freeman, the language arts teacher. All of the Tiger Team teachers were experienced professionals, with nearly sixty years of combined experience. All had been trained as secondary or high school teachers, but had chosen to remain in junior high schools and middle schools. They professed great love for the age group and thrived as teachers of preadolescent children.

The Tiger educational program was much more traditional than that of any other team in the school. The teachers reflected the belief that to facilitate learning, classrooms should be orderly and quiet, and they all used a positive but authoritarian approach to instruction and classroom management. Each teacher held his or her students to high standards of behavior and achievement, and the students responded well to the expectations. The classes were grouped by ability and prior achievement as well as behavior; there were four groups, including one "high," two "middle," and one "low" group. Although the students rarely worked in small groups or engaged in student-centered inquiry, the Tiger teachers were masters of whole-group instruction, and the students performed well.

Problems between the Lions and Tigers began shortly after a building addition forced the Lion Team to move to an area next to the Tigers. At first, the Tiger teachers calmly asked the Lion teachers to try to keep the Lion students quieter when they moved between classes; the noise was bothering the Tiger classes, which changed classes on a different schedule. However, even after the Lion teachers had spoken to the students, the noisiness generally returned to former levels very quickly. The Tiger teachers finally resorted to speaking with the principal about the noise, and she passed along the request to the Lion teachers. Clearly, the two teams of teachers had very different ideas as to what constituted too much noise. The Lion teachers spent a lot of time in the halls with the students between classes, frequently laughing and joking with them.

More problems began to occur as the Tiger teachers began to stop Lion students as they walked to the library; although the students always had written hall passes, the Tiger teachers usually made the students sit in the hall for up to thirty minutes while they returned to teaching their classes. Lisa, the Lion Team leader, approached Mark and politely asked that the Tiger teachers please send a note or let them know if a Lion student was disturbing their classes; the students, she said, were losing important library time while sitting in the hall. Mark agreed to send a note each time one of his team stopped a student, but the notes would arrive only after the offending student was released—around twenty to thirty minutes after being stopped. The Lion teachers then began to have their students walk around the building to get to the library; although this route took an additional couple of minutes, the problem appeared solved.

Tensions and animosities grew as the Lion teachers began to overhear colleagues talk about their "loose" ways. Many of the comments were critical of "liberal" or "progressive" notions that were being taught at universities.

The Lion Team decided on peace-making gestures: sending the Tiger teachers complimentary notes, writing commendation notes for Tiger students found doing exemplary chores or behaviors, and generally trying to be friendly and engaging. Most efforts were met with a distant coolness, and after several weeks of being friendly and receiving little in the way of reciprocity, the Lion teachers decided to simply ignore the Tiger Team and go on about their business of teaching.

On a rainy December day, the situation took a turn for the worse. Mildred caught a student from the Lion team sneaking down the Tiger hall; the student had been on his way to the library and was trying to avoid the cold rain by walking quietly but quickly through the Tiger hall. From her vantage point at the front of the room, Mildred saw the student; she yelled for him to stop, but the student ignored her and ran to the library. Mildred followed the boy, grabbed him by the shirt, and pulled him bodily back to the Lion hall, where she interrupted Mary's class and shouted, "This student is in more trouble than he can imagine; I'm going to see to it that he is suspended from school. Keep this one and all of your undisciplined monsters out of our hall."

Mary followed Mildred out of the room and tried to apologize to her, promising that the Lion students wouldn't use the hall. However, Mildred began to berate Mary, loudly exclaiming that none of the Lion teachers should be in education, that their "coddling" of the students was going to make them all criminals, and that the superintendent would hear about all this. Mary, young and untenured, began to cry just as the other Lion and Tiger teachers came into the hall. The situation was about to explode when the principal came around the corner.

Discussion Points

1. Although some details of this case may seem extreme, such situations arise frequently. What are the critical elements of this case?
2. What should the Lion Team do at this point?
3. Should the principal be involved? If so, how and in what role?
4. How might this type of situation affect the students?

The Case of the Wiped-Out Team

"**G**od, another group of visitors? Tomorrow?" Susie Petersen, the Star Team's math teacher, groaned. "I wish the office would shut down the visitors for awhile. They interrupt my classes, take valuable time from me and the kids, and sometimes I get the feeling that they don't believe me when I tell them how well this is working." She flopped down into the tattered, overstuffed chair in the corner of her room. Her team leader, Ron Phillips, pulled up a student chair and sat down.

"Yeah, I know. I asked the boss to let up for a while. He said he'd start sending the visitors to the Bears. Their grouping is working well, too." As he spoke, Angela Justis, the team's social studies teacher, came into the room.

"What? More visitors? Come on, Ron, this is getting out of hand." She pulled up a chair and continued, "That woman from County almost called me a liar last week. She didn't believe kids could make those kinds of improvements that quickly. She also told me to 'get a life' when I told her how much time we spent working up our groupings and developing assignments. She made me mad, and if the kids hadn't been there, I'd have given her a piece of my mind. She reminded me of some of my teachers in junior high school—you know the type."

"Yeah, she talked to me, too," admitted Ron. "But she's right about 'getting a life.' My wife told me that if I spent one more weekend here, she was going to leave me. I think she was kidding, but I'm not sure." Recalling the many Saturdays he had spent at the school holding computer classes for their students, he added, "I'm glad the kids are all pretty proficient with the hardware. But speaking of work, if I'm going to stay home this weekend, we've got to get some things done today. It's already four thirty, and I'm supposed to go to the board of education meeting tonight."

"Me, too, guys. I don't know if I can continue to do this. Nobody ever told me that teaching would be this much work. I even dream about this stuff at night. My husband says I should back off and play 'school' for a while—you know, put the desks in rows and give out worksheets." Susie rubbed her eyes as she spoke. "I'm pretty burned out."

"Hang in there, Suse, we've got seventy-eight seventh-graders who are having the best school year of their lives. Just think about Brandon—they almost retained him last year, and he just missed making the honor roll last six weeks," encouraged Ron.

"You're right, Ron. And I was sure scared of him at first. God, he's big! But it is a little easier now that we've got the computer stuff working," Susie replied. "Okay, I've got the math vocabulary words and the problems written out, but I haven't made the differentiated assignments yet. The kids were in here after school using the computer." She handed each of her teammates a copy.

The meeting continued, with the three Star teachers discussing the week's assignments, the various student groups that would be set up, and how each teacher's content could relate to another's. The team had had exceptional success with heterogeneous grouping and cooperative learning, but success had taken a toll on the members' energy and time. In the team's second year, visitors were an almost constant source of distraction. The work involved in regrouping students for each subsection of a content area or learning goal was time-consuming and often problematic. Nearly all of each teacher's work and plans was entered into a running computer log that Susie managed; the log also gave an annotated description of the student groups and their various assignments. The teachers often wrote their assignment sheets, contracts, and other worksheets on computers and used the technology to differentiate the assignments with respect to the students' abilities. They agreed that the team's success would have been impossible without the computers. Visiting teachers and administrators were often surprised at the extent of computer use on the Star Team. The team also used technology for students' independent exercises; students had been taught to use CD-ROM activities and word processing.

In addition, the three Star teachers had spent many days working together over the summer to develop their plans and activities. The other teams at the school were also having successes with heterogeneous grouping, but few were spending as much time and making as much of an effort as the Star Team. However, a planned thematic unit had been postponed indefinitely due to lack of time and energy. The scrutiny, recognition, and number of visitors they received were also beginning to cause some resentment among the faculty. It looked as though the Star Team was beginning to burn out.

Discussion Points

1. What can the team do at this point to alleviate the impending burnout?
2. The team's use of technology appears to be exemplary. In what other ways could the team use the technology to help solve their problems?
3. How could the team compensate for the resentment felt by the rest of the faculty?
4. What role should the principal have in helping this team?

The Case of the Inexperienced Teachers

The teams at Johnson Middle School had been formed during the summer before this school year. The job of putting the teams together was very difficult; the teachers gave their first, second, and third choices to the principal, John Jacobs, but the teachers' choices, certifications, subject areas, and levels of experience did not match the school's needs. Therefore, Mr. Jacobs's team designs were not quite what the teachers had expected, and he was prepared for some complaints. He was especially concerned with Ray Bernstein's seventh-grade team. Ray now sat in Mr. Jacobs's office, looking pensive and more than a little angry.

"I know it will be tough, Ray, but I'm counting on you to make this team work. All three of these teachers come with good qualifications and experience. Susan and Ann are especially good. Mike is a little young and hasn't had much middle school experience, but he's enthusiastic, and I hear he knows his stuff." The principal leaned toward Ray as he spoke.

"Much middle school experience? Mr. Jacobs, none of these teachers has ever taught this age group. Susan and Ann are high school teachers, for goodness' sake, and I hear they aren't real happy about coming up here anyway. And Mike . . . well, he did his student teaching in the fifth grade and last year he taught third! Why can't you spread them around a little and at least give me some people who know the age group?" Ray was known for his expertise with middle school kids and was considered an excellent teacher in the district.

"You know why, Ray. There is no other way I can match the certifications with the grade levels and subjects. I don't want to start this middle school organization in noncompliance with the state. And don't bother asking about provisional certificates; the office already warned me against that." The principal's voice had an edge and rose as he spoke.

"Okay, Mr. Jacobs, what do you suggest I do with these guys? Susan and Ann are already angry, and even though Mike is excited about coming here, he doesn't know anything about middle schools or preadolescent kids. I don't have the time to take them through a course in early adolescence or middle school curriculum. What about the thematic units you wanted us to do this year? These people are going to have a tough time getting through each day as it is. Piling a thematic unit on top of us isn't fair."

"Come on, Ray, you're grabbing at straws. Maybe a thematic unit is the way to get them going and to learn about these middle school kids . . . ."

"Right, and if you believe that I have a bridge I'd like to sell you," Ray interrupted.

"Okay, Ray, let's go over what you need to do to get them up to speed. You're concerned about Susan and Ann, so let's start with them. What can you do as team leader to help prepare them for our kids?" Mr. Jacobs ignored Ray's sarcasm and continued, "They'll need some of those materials about Piaget, Kohlberg, Erickson, Vygotsky, Bruner, and developmental stages, and they'll need some help with the physical and emotional stuff as well."

"Yeah, but will they read it? Even if they do read it, I'm afraid they won't buy into the ideas. I don't want to get stuck with another teammate who stands behind the lectern and lectures all day, every day, either. We'll have more discipline problems than ever before, and the kids won't learn anything. What about Howard Gardner's stuff about **multiple intelligences**? Shouldn't they have some of that, too? And what about the advisory program? Are they ready for that?" Ray was nearly whining, but Mr. Jacobs knew that he was close to convincing Ray that with a little work, Ray could shape the team and its instructional philosophy.

"They'll read it, Ray, and if you do the same stellar job with them that you did with the parents last year, you'll be there. Remember?"

Last year, Ray and the school's counselor had led a series of small workshops for parents about the developmental characteristics of middle school children, communicating with middle schoolers, and resolving conflicts. The workshops had started off small, but as word spread about how good they were, they not only filled up but had to be repeated to accommodate parents who had missed the first ones.

"I remember how much work that was, and how my wife was ready to shoot me for being away so much," Ray replied.

"Well, I think you might do some of the same stuff for your teammates," the principal suggested. "And I think I can get some extra pay for you and the team if you meet and work on this for a few days before the workdays in the fall."

"You owe me for this, Mr. Jacobs, and I'll remember it."

"Well, think of it this way, Ray. The kids will also thank you for this. The more these teachers know about middle school kids, the better off we'll all be."

Discussion Points

1. Middle school students are unique in many developmental ways. What are some of the developmental characteristics to which Ray Bernstein and Mr. Jacobs were referring?

2. Suggest some additional materials and activities that Ray might use with his new team.

3. What did Ray mean when he suggested that discipline problems were related to instructional strategies?

4. What are some characteristics of good middle school teachers, which Ray might hope to instill in his new team members?

References

Epstein, J., & MacIver, D. (1990). *Education in the middle grades: Overview of national practices and trends*. Columbus, OH: National Middle School Association.

Erb, T., & Doda, N. (1989). *Team organization: Promise, practices and possibilities*. Washington, DC: National Education Association.

3

CURRICULUM

The Case of the Unrealistic Expectations
The Case of the Unsuccessful Integrated Unit
The Case of Content Ignorance
The Case of the Book-Bound Teammate

IN ITS SIMPLEST FORM, middle school curriculum is the "what we learn" of education. Curriculum theorists and developers continue to debate what should be taught, who should control the curriculum, and to what extent students and teachers should be responsible and accountable for learning and teaching. While debates, discussions, and legislation continue, middle school teachers carry on with the tremendous job of developing and teaching a variety of curricula and content (Alexander & George, 1981; Beane, 1990).

It is becoming increasingly clear that interdisciplinary teams may afford the best potential for instructional relevance and rigor. Each member of a four-person team usually has expertise or certification in a particular content area (Erb & Doda, 1989). Many middle school teachers had undergraduate majors within one of the traditional subjects or disciplines. For most teachers educated in secondary education programs, a major area of study was generally required. The teams, therefore, should be replete with fairly special-

31

ized content knowledge, and thus should have the potential to bring about solid connections among the content areas.

The desire to make interdisciplinary connections, however, is often difficult to create and maintain. Teachers tend to rely on their experience with materials, resources, and texts to build each year's plan; even when mandates change the curricular aspects of a subject, teachers may continue to use many of the same materials in new contexts (Maeroff, 1993). Teachers should not be criticized too severely for this because the demands of developing good instruction and pedagogical content are extensive and complex. Teachers' content expertise is critical to the task of effective teaching and learning.

Exacerbating the complex task of curriculum development and delivery are the many factors that add to teachers' daily work. Schedules, even flexible ones, require constant monitoring and adaptation as the rhythms and exigencies of the schooldays fluctuate. Managing student behavior is a neverending task that can be emotionally debilitating. The complicated requirements for exceptional children increase the time and paperwork demands on teachers. Lack of planning and thinking time is the difficulty most frequently cited by teachers in middle schools. Therefore, even when they recognize the need for curriculum integration, lack of time can interfere with effectiveness. Other factors also play a role; for example, some teachers are unfamiliar with other content areas and hesitant to embark on a course that will take them into areas where they are uncomfortable.

The Case of the Unrealistic Expectations

"That's all there is to it," explained Bruce Mathews, principal of Liberty County Middle School. "You map out the concepts, tie them together, develop your activities, and as the TV commercial says, 'Just do it.'" Mr. Mathews was well known for his teaching skills and often ran his own staff development sessions for his school's fifty teachers. He had just returned from the state university, where he had attended a three-day seminar on developing thematic, integrated units for middle schools, and was presenting what he had learned to his staff. "Any questions?"

Tom Jensen, a middle-aged teacher, raised his hand. "This is all great, Bruce, but just when do we do all the planning this takes? It's only October and I don't know about the rest of the faculty, but I'm already behind. I haven't even started decimals yet, and this will put me even further behind. And you want us to do *two* of these things?"

"As I said, Tom, you can build your regular content into the unit. You said decimals? Well, for instance, you might use decimals a lot in, say, a unit on World War II. And you know how I am—I think depth is a lot more important than coverage of material." The principal paused, looked around the room, and said, "Everything is connected. We live in a connected world, and these kids need to see that. Three other principals and I developed a unit about rain forests during the workshop, and I relearned a lot of science and math that I hadn't used since grade school. Think about that, guys, three principals! And you know how ignorant principals are." There was scattered laughter around the room as he continued. "There's no rule that says a unit has to be two weeks long, either. It all depends on the unit. Some of the ones I saw were several weeks long and others were only a few days long."

Another hand was raised, and a young teacher, Penny Wilson, spoke up. "Mr. Mathews, I have a couple of the units I developed when I was in school, and I've never had a chance to try them out. Would it be okay if I did one of those?"

"Sure, Penny, but remember that this is a team effort. A good unit will make use of everyone's strengths. Just make sure that everybody's on the same page," the principal responded.

Betty McNeal was the next to speak. "Bruce, I don't want to sound like a nay-sayer, but I don't think my team could possibly pull this off this year. We have some of the toughest kids we've ever had, and just keeping up with them is taking all our time and effort. I'd feel a lot better if we took some time next summer and put something together. Maybe we could take a class or go to a workshop or conference."

"That's a good idea, Betty, and I have plans to send as many people as we can to the state middle school conference in March. But if we wait until March or next year, I'm afraid we'll run into the same problems."

More hands were raised, and several teachers began talking at once. Finally, a single voice was heard over the others as Harry Johnson spoke out. "Mr. Mathews, my wife Denise has had some experience with these over at Jackson School. She's done two or three of them, and let me tell you, they are a lot of work. And they cost money for extra materials. Is there any additional budget for this?"

"Not much, Harry, but there is some picture money left over, and I could help a little, but not much. Most of what you'll be doing won't cost anything but a little extra time. Could Denise help you with this?"

"I suppose, but with both of us teaching, we only see each other when we sit down and grade papers together. She's a math teacher. I don't know any math—that's why I became a social studies teacher!" Harry sat down, shaking his head.

More hands were raised, and the principal called on a middle-aged teacher, Gloria Rodriguez, who said, "I believe Harry has a good point. From what I've heard here and from what I've read and seen at conferences, integrated units often require a lot of extra knowledge in areas about which we know little to nothing. To ask us to do two of these this year means we'll have to do a lot of extra reading and preparation."

"Gloria, you're one of the best language arts teachers in the state. Your expertise would be critical to the success of any unit. I'm not asking you to go back to school, just to try this. Every unit will have a strong element of writing and reading, and that's where you come in. If the unit is about something in science, even, students will do a lot of reading and writing connected with the unit."

The meeting continued in a similar vein. Most of the teachers were hesitant and seemed to be resisting the idea. Bruce Mathews felt in his heart and mind that thematic, integrated units were the next step in his plan for the school. They had interdisciplinary teams, exploratories, advisory programs, and intramurals; integrated units seemed the natural next step in the progression.

Discussion Points

1. Which aspect of interdisciplinary thematic units seems to provoke the most resistance from the faculty? Why?

2. How much additional knowledge do the teachers need?

3. What could the principal have done differently in this meeting? What should his next steps be?

4. If you were a teacher in this school, what would you need before beginning to develop the units that the principal is requiring?

※ ※

The Case of the Unsuccessful Integrated Unit

The seventh-grade Beaver Team at Clear Spring Middle School was known for its expert teaching, child-centered climate, good parent relations, and team approach. The small school of 400 students had become a model for many other schools in the area with its team structure and successful students. The Beaver Team was often the object of other teams' envy, because the Beavers seemed to be successful at whatever educational endeavor they chose to undertake. It was at the end of the school year and the end of one of their most publicized activities that the team began to realize that although they were receiving a lot of publicity and recognition for their interdisciplinary activities and units, this year's seventh-grade students had done poorly on the end-of-year tests. This was the first year the team's students had not made significant gains on scores. The poor results came in spite of publicity and recognition for the Beaver Team's interdisciplinary activities and units. The team's dismay at the scores became evident during a team meeting near the end of the year.

"I don't understand it, George, I was certain that they would do better than this. I can't believe it. Our units included most of the state curriculum objectives, and we always stressed them. I thought this group of Beavers was one of the best we've ever had." Marlene Garvey sighed as she slumped in her chair in her classroom. "All that work, all those plans, all that publicity. I'm embarrassed, especially after the TV station did all that coverage for the Greece unit. What do you think the parents will do when they see these scores?"

"Well, not everybody went down. And they really didn't go down so much as slide a little," replied George Strait, the team leader. "Our Beaver parents have always been super supportive to the limit. I don't know what to say to them, either."

"Well, maybe we ought to spend some time this summer looking at our curriculum," suggested Riley White, the math teacher on the team. "I know there wasn't much math in the Greece unit. Maybe we need to go back to the old way of doing things. You know, we did a lot of those units this year—six if you count the light and sound unit. The kids did well on the test on that stuff, though, didn't they?"

"Yeah, they did. I wonder why?" asked Patricia Simpson, the science teacher. "We really didn't do a lot differently, did we? I mean, we planned the unit the same way we did the others, mapping out the concepts, skills, and knowledge we wanted the kids to know, and went from there. And that was the first one we did, wasn't it?"

"Let's think about that," suggested Marlene. "What is there about the light and sound unit that's different from the Greece unit? Besides the publicity, of course. Nobody much cared about the science stuff—too ordinary, I guess. There sure wasn't any TV or newspaper coverage!"

"Okay, I have the plans right here," replied Patricia, as she spread her dog-eared photocopies across the table for the team to see.

"Well, I can't see much difference, people—the steps are the same," Riley said.

"Yeah, but there is a difference," noted George. "See? There must be three times as much active, hands-on stuff in the Greece unit. See what I mean? Here's where we did the costumes for the gods and goddesses, and here are the skits, and here's the sculpture, and. . . ."

"Wait," Patricia said. "Look at our goals and objectives for the Greece unit—did we really meet those? I mean, we have objectives that read like a curriculum guide, but how did the skit contribute to them? And if you look at the goals and objectives for the light and sound unit, we met most of those. Yeah, there's a lot of fun stuff in both of them, and maybe the stuff in the Greece unit is more fun, but it sure didn't help us meet the goals."

"Yeah, Patricia, maybe that's it. We kind of got carried away with all the glitzy stuff as the year went on," suggested Riley. "I mean we wrote some good math objectives for the Greece unit, but we didn't do much with them except some worksheets and puzzles. There was plenty of math in the light and sound unit, and our hands-on stuff was tied directly to the concepts and not just stuffed into the unit. I'm embarrassed. What fools we've been."

"Maybe, but let's not jump to conclusions too quickly. What about all the other units we did—rain forests, Native Americans, and the others. Those were pretty good, weren't they?"

Discussion Points

1. The problem here is a very common and obvious one. How could it be restated?
2. What resources are available to ensure the content and intellectual validity of a thematic unit?
3. What checks and balances might be implemented as a unit takes place?
4. What implications does this case have for cross-content knowledge?
5. What does this case say about the type of culminating activities that should be associated with a thematic unit?

The Case of Content Ignorance

The Madison Middle School staff and faculty had experienced a great deal of change and reassignment since the school had adopted the "middle school philosophy" three years ago. Indeed, none of the teams still consisted of the same members from the first year. Among the members of the Superior Team, Beth Lanning, a math teacher, and Sharon Pepper, a science teacher, had had one year together. This year, the team had added Barry Miller for social studies and Linda Larson for language arts. All the teachers, however, knew each other well, having taught together in various capacities for more than ten years. Sharon had the least teaching experience—three years—and all the others had more than ten years' experience each.

Beth, Sharon, and Linda often expressed a strong interest in developing integrated, thematic units of instruction, and during one social event they had been able to sketch out a science unit about a topic of common interest, technology. After that informal meeting, Beth, the team leader, had written out a comprehensive set of plans for a fifteen-day unit that would coincide with the students' computer exploratory class. During the unit, the students would have the opportunity to work with computers, telecommunications, network databases, and other technology available on the school premises. The three teachers had posed the idea of the unit to their colleague Barry before school started, and he had appeared excited about the unit, saying that this experience would allow him to learn about computers, too.

As the school year began, the four teachers spent long hours developing goals, objectives, activities, evaluations, and speakers for the unit that was to take place during the second nine-week grading period, which would begin near the end of October. The exploratory teacher took part in much of the planning, and the principal often took the opportunity to remind the rest of the faculty that the team's activities were appreciated. As the end of October approached, the team was excited about the unit.

Problems began to surface almost immediately. Barry's role was to provide a set of meaningful activities that showed the students how technology—past, present, and current—affected society. He had planned to show videotapes, do several simulations and role-plays, and visit a regional science museum, as well as provide interesting reading materials. The teachers and the students soon began to notice that Barry was unable to answer any of the students' questions. Further, the activities, readings, and written work were often left ungraded. Indeed, some of the grading was wrong: Barry had marked students' work incorrect when it was indeed correct. Then the students complained that if they were required to use a word processor for all their work, Barry should be required to use one for his assignments as well.

Two parents called the team and complained when Barry allegedly made incorrect statements in class about the history of technology during the Renaissance. After the first week, Beth broached the subject with Barry after the schoolday, in the privacy of his classroom.

"Barry, a couple of parents called yesterday about your class. You know how they can be. They were concerned about some of the things you said about the unit. Just thought I'd let you know."

"Oh, yeah? Well, I might have said a couple of things that I didn't check first. Sorry—I haven't had much time to do all of the reading that this thing takes. Should I call them?"

"No, I think it's settled. How's it going? Can I help you with anything? I know this stuff is as unfamiliar to you as it is to us, but it's fun, don't you think?" Beth asked.

"Yeah, I guess. It's sure different not having a book to use. It's hard to plan out how long stuff takes. Today, I ran out of material in the first fifteen minutes of class. Had to wing it," Barry responded.

"Well, we're meeting this afternoon during team planning period. See you there."

During the meeting, Barry seemed distant and uncomfortable as his teammates enthusiastically discussed the unit. With the exception of Barry's problem, the students were working eagerly and learning beyond the teachers' expectations.

"I can't believe it. Susan Potter actually wrote a three-page, word-processed report," Linda said. "It's the first good work she's done all year. This is great! All that work and reading is worth it!"

"I think we should shut it down. Now." Barry's words hung in the room like a cloud.

"You're kidding, of course," replied Sharon. "This is the most fun I've had teaching in years!" When she realized that Barry was serious, she asked, "What's going on, Barry?"

"This stuff is worthless. The tests at the end of the year don't cover any of this stuff, I think it's boring, and too much work, and I hate computers, anyway," Barry responded. "It's worthless," he repeated. "They won't remember any of it."

"Wait a minute, Barry," Beth interjected. "I realize this isn't your cup of tea, but I disagree. The kids are learning, and they're writing more than ever, and the math part has them thinking about something besides how to divide fractions, and your part is really important. They need to know how all of this has changed society and how it will change their world in future. What do you mean, it's worthless?"

"I'm sorry, but tomorrow, I'm going back to the textbook. I'm too far behind as it is."

Discussion Points

1. What appears to be the central problem in this case?
2. How could Beth and the team work with Barry?

3. What types of content might be helpful for Barry to use in this case?
4. What steps might have been taken to prevent this problem?
5. Would choosing another topic have led to different or better results?

The Case of the Book-Bound Teammate

The classroom was in what would be a normal state of disarray at the end of a day at Lee Middle School. Scraps of paper were strewn around the room, the books that once had been neatly stored in the bookcases were now haphazardly placed, the desks that had been neatly arranged in groups of three or four were now pushed around in different parts of the room, and two desks had forgotten bookbags stored underneath them. Maria Romero's desk was piled high with papers, books, a volume from an encyclopedia, two dictionaries, an almanac, and several other large reference books. On one side of the room, a long shelf was labeled with an obviously student-made sign that said "Student Projects—Do Not Touch." Along the shelf were the beginning stages of dioramas, more reference books, a slide projector, and a stack of videotapes. To the left of the shelf was a table that held a computer with a CD player and a printer. The computer was off, but someone had left a compact disc on top of the monitor. Maria sighed, picked up the CD, moved a few books and papers, located the box for the CD, and snapped it into place. As she looked around the room, her classroom door opened, and one of her teammates, Rosalyn Perkins, came in.

"Wow, looks like the guys had a field day in here, Maria," she laughed. She knew, however, that within a few minutes the room would be clear of any trash, the books would be restored to their proper place, and a large canvas bag would hold most of the work on Maria's desk. Maria and Rosalyn both spent a great deal of time at home assessing and evaluating student work.

"I just hope it's worth it," murmured Maria. "They are really doing good work on their social studies projects, and I am certain that they are learning a lot more doing things this way than reading it from a text. You should have seen Michelle today! She put together a file of political cartoon images and newspaper editorials from one of the CDs that illustrates some of the points we're trying to make about the beginnings of World War II. Pretty good for a girl who reads at about a third-grade level."

"I know, she was talking about it in my class this afternoon. She's going to write an editorial of her own for her weekly writing log," answered Rosalyn.

"I think the kids understand more about what led up to the war than I did when I was in college—and I was a history major!"

"Well, I hate to bust your bubble, but our resident curriculum expert thinks you are wasting time. Olivia was complaining to the principal this afternoon about how you are behind in the book."

"What did she say?" Maria asked, looking confused and concerned. "I thought she supported this. She was the one who brought back all that stuff from the conference about depth of content versus breadth of content."

"I know, but she told the principal that you were at least three months behind in the curriculum, and she was worried that the kids weren't going to get enough knowledge to be able to perform next year when they go to high school," responded Rosalyn. "You know how her husband complains about the middle school. He teaches those two tough advanced-placement history classes at Franklin High that the school board is always talking about."

"Well, I think our kids are getting a much richer and more meaningful base of social studies, especially early twentieth-century U.S. history, than those that are just reading chapters and answering questions," Maria said defensively. "Besides, there aren't many of our kids who will ever take those AP classes. I'm more interested in having our kids come away with understanding—not just a bunch of facts and dates that they'll never remember."

"Well, I thought you'd like to know what she is saying. Are you going to talk with her?"

"I guess so. After all, she is the team leader, and she's also chair of the math department. I'll have to be careful though—she can get pretty defensive herself," answered Maria.

"Well, I have to go to the dentist, so I can't hang around. Let me know what happens, okay?" said Rosalyn as she moved toward the door and left the room.

Maria was worried. She thought she was getting along well with Olivia this year, but she realized now that they had not discussed curriculum at all in the team meetings since Olivia had given them copies of some articles and handouts she had collected at a conference. The school district had a curriculum guide, but few faculty members here at Lee seemed to follow it. The central office curriculum supervisors did not mention it very often, unless the subject came up at one of the infrequent district professional development workshops. The main issues during the last school board election had been salaries and administrative waste, so Maria felt that the board members weren't too interested in curriculum matters, either. However as she continued to reflect about the curriculum, she realized that most of the teachers here at Lee Middle School typically followed the adopted textbooks. Until last year, when she had convinced the team to do a thematic unit about cultures around the world, she herself had followed the textbooks' scope and sequence of content. Over the summer, Maria had developed a comprehensive social studies unit centered on conflict that had grown out of the cultures unit, and it was this unit that had taken so much time. She remained convinced, though, that the students were not only enjoying the content more, they were reaching much deeper levels of understanding about it.

She was afraid of Olivia's response. Maria had less experience than Olivia, and she knew that Olivia had very strong connections to the principal and other administrators. She dreaded the thought of a confrontation.

Discussion Points

1. What issues related to middle level curriculum are involved in this case?

2. What evidence could Maria produce that might convince her colleagues that her approach is valuable and worthwhile?

3. No mention was made of standardized tests in this case, but this type of testing is often used when presenting curriculum arguments. What are some curriculum issues that might emerge regarding testing of middle school students?

4. How do you perceive the operational effectiveness of this team? What sorts of team activities or directions might help the team with curriculum issues?

References

Alexander, W. M., & George, P. S. (1981). *The exemplary middle school.* New York: Holt, Rinehart & Winston.

Beane, J. A. (1990). *A middle school curriculum: From rhetoric to reality.* Columbus, OH: National Middle School Association.

Erb, T. O., & Doda, N. M. (1989). *Team organization: Promise, practices and possibilities.* Washington, DC: National Education Association.

Maeroff, G. L. (1993). *Team building for school change: Equipping teachers for new roles.* New York: Teachers College Press.

❧ 4 ❧

INSTRUCTION

The Case of the Stubborn Teachers
The Case of the Cognitive Soup
The Case of the Difficult Student Grouping
The Case of the Mad Mom
The Case of Techno-Literacy

INSTRUCTION IN THE middle grades is often an eclectic assortment of practices taken from both the early grades and high school. Instructional practices for middle school students, however, need to be firmly grounded in what we know about how these students learn (Stevenson, 1992). This is not an easy or simple task, since middle schoolers learn in a variety of ways and styles; they move inconsistently from concrete to abstract ways of thinking (Kellough & Kellough, 1996). Thus, the best instructional practices make use of a variety of instructional methods that range from hands-on exploratory activities to brief lectures and note taking. These practices, however, must be carefully applied and pedagogically sound. The use of a single type of instructional method to the exclusion of all others is not only unwarranted but also can be counterproductive.

It is in the area of instructional methods that good middle school leadership becomes critical, and the leadership must come both formally from administrators and informally from peers. Again, interdisciplinary teams can help provide the support structures and peer coaching that are often needed when teachers change methods or attempt new practices.

Careful student grouping is also a necessity. Too often, middle school teachers and administrators pay scant attention to the complexities of grouping students, particularly when they are under pressure to reduce tracking and other forms of ability grouping. To group students properly for instruction or team assignment, one must know them well. This knowledge of the students must go beyond summary scores from a standardized test to include extensive understanding of the students' backgrounds, learning modes, trouble spots, and, in many cases, family histories. Even when grouping has been completed in a careful and appropriate manner, the instructional methods used for the groups must be further tailored to meet the students' and teachers' learning needs (Erb & Doda, 1989). Cooperative learning means much more than simply putting a high achieving student, a low achieving student, and a couple of average students together in a group.

Curriculum, instruction, and classroom strategies must also be carefully investigated and applied to make use of the students' strengths and to work on weaknesses. For example, a common mistake that teachers make in the design of a thematic, **interdisciplinary unit** is to emphasize the accumulation of factual material. Facts learned in a thematic unit may be retained for a longer period of time, but unless they are combined with higher order thinking and problem solving in a real and relevant context, facts eventually slip away (Ackerman, 1989).

Evaluation and assessment are closely tied to instruction. Cooperative group learning must be assessed differently than individual learning: in group learning situations, processes, thinking, and communication of ideas are critical, and these elements often are not evaluated. The notion of authentic assessment is extremely important in middle level education, as problem-solving relevance brings concreteness to abstract problems and applications (Zessoules & Gardner, 1991).

❧ ❧

The Case of the Stubborn Teachers

Central Middle School had formerly been Central High School, and the old building had high ceilings and wide halls. The surrounding neighborhood was deteriorating somewhat, as the middle-class inhabitants moved to the suburbs. However, low-income and immigrant families found fairly inexpensive housing in the area, so the school's enrollment continued to grow.

The principal of the middle school, John Wimer, had successfully led two other schools in the district from junior high school models to middle school models. The teachers were on interdisciplinary teams, but the team concept had not yet taken a firm hold, primarily because nearly half the teachers in the school had remained at Central when the new high school had opened. Those teachers, who had formerly taught ninth through twelfth grades, had not been selected to go to the new high school.

Dr. Wimer's systematic staff development activities had been going on for two years. They covered most aspects of middle school teaching, including developmental characteristics of students, pre- and early adolescent cognitive science and learning theories, interdisciplinary thematic unit development, and the instructional strategies connected to these ideas. However, the teachers remained loyal to a lecture-notes-test format, and the principal was very concerned about this. The teachers with elementary school backgrounds did very well with middle school strategies, but those who had taught high school were reluctant to try new ideas. Exacerbating the situation was the fact that student grades were quite high. Indeed, the honor roll each six weeks was longer than any Dr. Wimer had ever experienced. He was extremely frustrated as he visited classrooms and made formal and informal evaluation observations. The classrooms appeared well organized and functional, but students were invariably sitting in rows, taking notes, and doing worksheets. The level of questioning was low, consisting primarily of knowledge and comprehension questions; students memorized lists, dates, and definitions and were tested on their recall. John knew that little of the material would be retained for very long. When he discussed his concerns during postobservation conferences, the teachers seemed to rely on their grade books and lack of discipline problems as measures of their students' success. Each conference seemed to end with promises to try some cooperative groups or projects, but the promises proved to be empty.

The principal's concerns and suspicions grew after speaking with two different parents about minor discipline problems. One of the parents commented that she was very surprised at her son's behavior, especially since his grades were so much better than before—nearly all As and Bs. The other parent expressed some concern that even though the family spoke some English at home, as well as Spanish, his son was still having a great deal of trouble reading English. Yet he was getting Bs and Cs in language. He wanted to know if the school could offer his son some extra help with English.

Dr. Wimer made his concerns known during the next regularly scheduled faculty meeting. There were two items on the agenda: announcements and instruction. The announcements took only a couple of minutes, then the principal smiled and began, "You are about to take a test. Please get out a pencil and clear your table. There are ten items on this test, and I can assure you that these are items that you have seen before. In fact, I'd bet that all of you have answered these questions correctly at least once before, so this shouldn't be difficult. When you are ready, I'll pass the test papers out." He paused, and several teachers' hands shot up into the air. One sixth-grade teacher, Richard Lopez, didn't wait to be called on and loudly asked, "Will we be graded on a curve?"

Most of the teachers laughed, and the principal's smile faded as he replied, "No, Richard, each question is worth ten points and you must get a seventy to pass." Several teachers laughed, but softly, as they began to be concerned about this task.

The test questions ranged from the definition of *standard deviation* to historical dates. There was audible mumbling as the teachers began to take the test. Several hands were raised again, and one teacher asked, "How specific do these answers have to be? I mean, I know about when the Sistine Chapel was painted, but I don't know the exact date it was finished." Dr. Wimer replied, "As specific as you can be. Please hurry, you have only ten more minutes to complete the quiz."

At the end of ten minutes, the principal asked that the papers be handed up to him. As the teachers complied, Richard asked, "John, what's this about? Are we on *Candid Camera*?"

"Okay, you've been good sports about this, so I'll tell you what I have in mind. I am concerned about the learning that is taking place in some of our classes. I know you all probably remember Bloom's taxonomy, and I'm worried that most, if not all, of the types of things we are teaching are low level—knowledge and comprehension. I'd like to discuss with you some ways to reach higher levels of thinking without jeopardizing the progress of our minority or immigrant students. Here's what I have in mind."

Discussion Points

1. What do you think Dr. Wimer has in mind, and how effective do you think his plan will be?

2. Explain where you think the problem lies in this case.

3. If the former high school teachers are the only problem, why did Dr. Wimer give his "test" to all the teachers? Is this a good strategy?

4. Resistance to an innovation often masks implementation problems. What are the primary causes of the resistance in this case?

The Case of the Cognitive Soup

Baker Middle School was a magnet school for the medium-sized city in which it was located. Its theme and major focus was math and science, and students were bused to the school from all over the district. Children who lived in the neighborhood, however, were allowed to attend without restrictions, and this open enrollment resulted in crowded classrooms. The school leadership consisted of the principals and team leaders, and during the previous year they had decided to spend almost all the staff development funds for teacher training in learning styles, forms of intelligence, preadolescent cognitive development, and instructional differentiation. Indeed, all the teachers had participated in a full week of classes during the summer to learn about these alternatives and how to use them in their classes. This year, most of the teachers had begun implementing a variety of strategies that they hoped would help them improve their instruction, and in most cases, the cautious application of the strategies seemed to be working.

Patricia Hobbs, however, was having her doubts as to the effectiveness of these strategies. Pat taught sixth-grade math and for years had been looked upon as one of the best math teachers in the district. During the past four months she had implemented hands-on approaches to math instruction, using the National Council of Teachers of Mathematics (NCTM) standards; she had also varied her instructional tactics and tried to provide for the many learning styles found on her team. In the process she had found that most of the students' grades had declined—some severely.

This Tuesday was no different. In her classes about dividing decimals, Pat used "ten-blocks" and an overhead projector to demonstrate the rules about putting the decimal in its correct place, and she also allowed students to work in small groups on the floor. The results of the quiz at the end of the period were terrible. Most of the students had some idea of how to do the calculation, but few of them could do it consistently without error, particularly if the problems deviated from a standard form. Pat found herself thinking that her "old" way of teaching these strategies had been far more successful.

After school, during the regularly scheduled team meeting, Pat shared her concern with her colleagues. "I'm having trouble making all of this new stuff work, my friends. And I don't know if it's my fault or if the process simply doesn't work as well as the way I used to do it. I have more kids with Ds than I have ever had by this time of the year, and I'm scared they won't do very well on the end-of-year tests."

"What are you using?" asked Jerry Smith, the science teacher.

"Well, I'm using small groups, hands-on demonstrations, and problem solving. I'm trying to keep soft music playing in the class—classical, of course—and I'm trying to make sure that the kids who are spatially intelligent are seeing how these rules fit together," she responded.

"All of that at once?" asked Jerry.

"Yeah, well, it's not that difficult to actually do. One problem is the planning it takes for the spatial learners, but the worst is the noise and messing around in the groups. I'm still seeing one or two kids in a group doing most of the work and the others sort of copying things down. But that's what the consultant said would happen, and she said the others will eventually pick it up. It's just that they aren't."

"Would you like me to come and watch tomorrow?" asked Jerry, "I'll have Rose give the test for me, and I'll sit in on the class."

"I'll be nervous, Jerry—you know how I am about visitors—but that's okay. Let's give it a try."

Wednesday's class seemed fairly typical, according to Pat. Jerry visited, sitting in the rear of the room for most of the time, but getting up and helping the students when he saw it was needed. The class began with Pat reviewing what the students had done the day before, and then she used the overhead to give a demonstration with ten-blocks. She kept the radio on for the entire period, and she spent five or six minutes talking about the spatial relationships in the ten-blocks. She then passed out a worksheet for the groups, and they tackled it, using calculators to check their work.

After ten minutes or so, two of the groups had finished and were busily talking and laughing. The remaining groups had not finished, and one group was having an especially difficult time with the assignment. Pat approached Jerry and said, "See? It's like this every day. Look, Tommy's group is finished, and so is Maria's. But Edwina's group seems to be lost and they are trying to copy Tommy's group's work."

After twenty minutes on the assignment, Pat told the students to go back to their seats and work on the sheet alone. However, the damage had been done, and the class continued to be unruly and noisy.

After school that day, Jerry and Pat met to discuss the class.

"Well, I told you it was a zoo. How bad am I?" Pat asked.

"You aren't bad, Pat, but the kids were plenty goofy today. I saw lots of good things happening. The groups were noisy, but most of them were getting it. Maybe if you just made the time they work in groups shorter . . . ."

Discussion Points

1. What are some of the instructional problems evident in this case?
2. What areas of implementation of the innovations seem to be problematic?
3. What steps should Pat take next?
4. What role should the interdisciplinary team play in this case?
5. How might the problems of implementing innovative or new practices be avoided and/or overcome?

The Case of the Difficult Student Grouping

Beacon Middle School housed more than a thousand sixth-, seventh-, and eighth-grade students and had more than eighty faculty members, including three counselors and two assistant principals. The principal, Donna Spence, had been hired from a neighboring district, primarily because of her expertise with heterogeneous grouping and her prior successes with similar situations. Although the school was located in the central part of a city of 75,000 inhabitants, nearly half the students were bused to the school from other areas of the city. The busing had been implemented to accommodate a federal order to balance the racial disparities in the area. In addition, the school was under federal orders to group students so as to eliminate any tracking that would result in minority or low-income students being grouped together. The administration and school board ordered the school to cease ability grouping and to group students heterogeneously.

To its credit, the district administration had paid a substantial amount to train all of Beacon's teachers in alternative methods of instruction. The training included a three-day workshop on cooperative learning. The school district also hired three additional teachers whose role, besides being classroom teachers, was to provide leadership and assistance to other teachers as they began the process of teaching in heterogeneous groups. One of these "lead" teachers was assigned to each grade level.

Three years earlier the previous school leadership had decided to implement interdisciplinary teams and an **advisor-advisee program** for teachers. Teams had been in place for those three years, but their members had continued to operate much as they had when the school was a junior high school.

The teacher advisory program, known as the TLC Program, was commercially produced. The funds to purchase the program had been acquired through a grant from a local business consortium that often supported schools' efforts. It had not been very successful: the commercial materials were expensive, difficult to use, and consisted of mostly paper-and-pencil tasks and open-ended questions for discussion. Use of the program, therefore, had gradually diminished to the point where most teachers used the twenty-five-minute period for free time or as time when students could do homework. The only benefit from the program, it seemed, was the increased completion of homework in the classes.

Through the first two months of the school year, behavior problems increased dramatically. Fights took place almost daily, and the in-school suspension room was constantly full. Students, especially those of lower ability and achievement, were disruptive in class and often refused to do the assigned work. It was not uncommon for students to sleep in class, while teachers ignored them and continued their instruction. Cooperative groups were in place in nearly all the classes, but it seemed that only the higher achieving students completed the work, and the parents of these students often complained that their children were doing the work of the teachers in the groups.

Teacher morale at the beginning of the year had been fairly high, but it had dropped steeply as the problems became pervasive. By the beginning of October, teacher absenteeism was sharply higher than in the past, and two teachers had already resigned.

At the end of the first six-week grading period, nearly three-fourths of the students had at least one failing grade on their report cards, and more than 25 percent had three failing grades.

The problems on the Jaguar Team seemed to reflect what was happening all over the school. During one of the regular team meetings, Marcia Bryant, the team leader, shared her frustrations with her teammates and the principal. "I've been teaching fifteen years, gang, and this has got to be the worst. At least last year I only had one period of kids who drove me crazy. This year it's all day, every period. They aren't learning any math at all, and this cooperative learning is so noisy I'm going nuts." Nearly in tears, she continued, "Donna, I know you and the other principals are doing all you can, but something's got to change."

"I know, Marcia, it's tough, but we knew this year would be a difficult one," Donna replied. "All I ask is that you hang in there, and we'll do all we can to support you. Your team has a particularly tough bunch of kids, and you may not realize it, but you're doing great. Look what's happened with Jeffrey—he's having the best school year he's ever had."

"Yeah, we know," responded Tim Weaver, the team's science teacher. "But for every Jeffrey, there are about fifty others who are screwing up. What we'd like, Donna, is to change some of our classes. You know, regroup a few of the kids to at least separate the squirrels, like Sharon and Lisa. Those two are like oil and water, and it seems like every day they're at each other's throats."

"Hold off for a while, Tim," answered Donna. "I don't think we should move any kids just yet. If we do that, we open the floodgates, and that means trouble." She continued, "I've scheduled some more workshops for next month. There's a special education professor from the university who is coming to do a series about behavior management. I think he'll help a lot. His name is Reed, and I've read some of his articles, and they're good."

"Oh my, Donna, I had him for a class last year. He's one of those 'listen to their feelings' guys, and I don't think he's been in a classroom for a million years," replied Lauren LaRosa, the language arts teacher. She rolled her eyes and went on, "We don't need workshops, we need to move some of these kids. I've got kids who can't read at all with kids who could do high school work. I spend all my time with the nonreaders and ignore the high kids. It isn't fair!"

"Give it a chance, Lauren," Donna said. "It's only the first of October, and this kind of thing doesn't improve overnight."

"That's what worries me, Donna, that's what worries me," Tim responded. "It's going to be the longest year of my life."

Discussion Points

1. As terrible as this situation sounds, it is not uncommon. What are the central problems at Beacon?
2. As a team member, what would steps would you propose to take?
3. If you were the principal, how might you respond to this situation?
4. What elements are present in the school that might lead to improvement in the situation?

The Case of the Mad Mom

"If this is not changed, I'm afraid I'll have to go to the school board." Ms. Mathers's voice was high with tension and anger. "This simply isn't fair. Jonathan is gifted, and that shouldn't be a reason for you to take advantage of him. He doesn't need to do a lot of that busy work you give the groups. He's bored, and he's not learning anything new." She leaned forward in her chair, frowning at the three teachers at the table.

"Ms. Mathers, I'm sorry you feel that way, and if it will make you feel better, we won't have Jonathan do any more tutoring. But he will have to remain in the groups; he needs to learn how to work in groups, and he seems to like it. Maybe we could give him some additional work to do in class." Becky Smith's voice was shaking as she spoke. She was the Rabbit Team leader, and she was tired and angry. Besides, she knew that these types of confrontations stuck in her mind for days.

"You aren't hearing me, Ms. Smith," Ms. Mathers replied. "I will not have him working in those groups any longer. I will not place him in a situation where someone else can affect his grades. That, too, is not fair. And he learned how to work in groups, as you call it, in kindergarten. He's in the sixth grade now, and with his ability, he should be challenged, not punished." She too, now appeared near tears, her voice trembling. "I'm not asking much, but should this continue, I'll have no choice. I'm trying to be fair; that's why I came to you first."

"We know that, Ms. Mathers," responded John Taylor, the team's language arts teacher. "We appreciate that. Jonathan is a great kid and we all like him a lot. We want what's best for him, too. We aren't using any groups in language arts, and he's a great writer. It's a pleasure to have him in my class." He sat back in his chair.

"He told me you were using peer editing. Isn't that groups?" Ms. Mathers asked.

"Well, we edit each other's papers, much as you would do if he brought a paper home to you. But there's no grading involved, and the end result is better writing for all of us," John explained.

"I can handle that, Mr. Taylor, but that's different from the math and science and social studies. As I understand it, group grades are given that can affect a student's final grade. Isn't that true?" She turned to Becky.

"Well, yes, in a way. But the group grades are weighted so that only a very small portion of that grade counts toward the final grade," Becky explained. "The group grade is the incentive for working together. My math classes are able to handle much more complex problems when they work together."

"You call those complex? Jonathan can do those problems in his sleep! And from what he tells me, he does the problems and the others copy the answers. This is not fair, and it is a travesty of what you call education!" Ms. Mathers was now nearly yelling as she gathered her coat and purse. "You leave me no choice." She rose and left the classroom, and the team could hear her steps fading down the hall.

"Well? What do you think?" Becky asked.

For the first time during the meeting, Patrick O'Hara spoke. "She's mad, that's for sure. I doubt whether she'll go to the board, but I wouldn't be surprised if she went to Mr. Kramer. And as much as he wants us to use cooperative learning, he'll bend over backward for her. She can be a pain in the you-know-what."

"Well, she was a pain today, that's for sure!" Becky said emphatically. "And you know, as much as I hate to say it, she has a point. I'm kind of tired of the groups, too. They're noisy, too few kids do any work, and the kids couldn't care less about the group grades."

"Well, the groups I use in writers' workshop sure work. The kids are doing better than I had hoped," John replied. "But this could turn into something serious. Over at Midtown Middle, there was a group of parents of gifted kids that practically ran off the principal and a bunch of her teachers. I know that school is in the county system, and they have more gifted students than we do, but the Matherses have always been pretty vocal and involved parents. They could stir up trouble. If I were you, Becky, I'd talk to Kramer. We need to cover ourselves. If he wants us to do this stuff, he's going to have to back us up." As he spoke, he gathered up his grade book and headed for the door.

Discussion Points

1. Should bright or gifted students be used as tutors or leaders in groups? Why or why not?

2. What steps could be taken to accommodate Ms. Mathers's wishes and remain true to the team's goals of using cooperative groups?

3. There are hints of other problems in this case. What are they, and what steps should be taken?

4. What supportive roles might the principal play in this conflict?

The Case of Techno-Literacy

Mildred Martin's hand was perceptibly shaking as she moved the computer mouse around on the soft plastic pad next to the computer. She placed the pointer on one of the icons and was pleased to hear the quiet whir of the compact disc seeking its spot. However, the image on the screen bore no resemblance to what Mildred had wanted to see. She muttered something and repeatedly clicked on one of the other menu items that ran across the top of the screen. She continued, angrily clicking on menu items until the computer finally stopped responding and signaled her with a series of beeps. "I don't understand why it worked then and not now," she said to herself as she turned the machine off and left the computer lab. As she went out, she spoke softly to one of her former students who was seated at a nearby computer, saying, "Hope you have better luck than I did, Mary."

Later that day the members of Mildred's team were seated in the planning room, and when she entered, Rodney Williams, the team's science teacher, asked, "Well, Mildred, how did it go? Did you get it to sit up and beg?"

Mildred put her hands on her hips and said disgustedly, "No, Rod, computers and I still aren't on speaking terms. Can you help me with this stuff after school? I have to pass the district test this year or they'll be sending me back to the first grade where everybody is computer literate."

The district had recently adopted a leveled set of technology literacy tests that all teachers were required to pass; each level was more difficult and complex than the one before, and involved more exacting types of software. Level one, the test that Mildred had yet to pass, covered handling diskettes, using a mouse, opening software packages, setting up simple grade book and grade averaging files, using a mouse or keyboard to view slides or graphics from a CD, and demonstrating elementary word-processing skills. Levels two and three included more difficult programs, all the way to setting up a relational database. Every teacher had two years to pass level one and then had to pass levels two and three within the next two years.

Mildred's team was considered one of the best at Venture Middle School. All the teachers were middle school veterans who seemed to love their chosen work; they had all been educated in middle school curriculum and instruction. The team's teaching philosophy had a fairly traditional flavor, but all four members used a variety of methods, including cooperative groups, hand-on activities, and three or four extensive integrated thematic units each year. Most of the teachers' content and subject matter were taken directly from either the state mandates or textbooks. The use of technology, however, was notably absent on the team, among both teachers and students. Rodney was the only teacher who used a computer to write tests or handouts; he was also the only one who used a simple grade book program to manage his students' grades. In fact, it was well known at Venture that the team members were not only fearful of computers but openly antagonistic toward technology and those who used it. The team members had often taken good-natured teasing during faculty meetings about their noted opposition to computers and technology.

"Well, teammates, I think the time has come for us to either get on the bandwagon or throw in the towel," Rodney said, leaning back in his chair.

"If we don't learn how to do these things, we are going to be in trouble, and I am beginning to think that our students are already suffering because we use and require so little technology in our classes. Our kids get to the computer lab once a week, but most of what they are doing, I think, is playing games and doing remedial work. Some of the girls are also complaining that the boys take more time than they do."

"Well, I still think that computers will never replace old-fashioned good teaching," Regina Taylor, the team's language arts teacher, said disgustedly. "I wouldn't be surprised if someday kids won't even learn cursive—they'll just learn to use a keyboard. I think it's a shame that we have come to this, but if the administration wants me to pass the test, then I'll learn the stuff and pass the test. I've been doing that kind of thing all my life."

"We each have a computer in our rooms, but we hardly ever use them," Rodney said. "Maybe I should take some time and show you guys what I use mine for. But I'll warn you, I don't know very much. I doubt if I can pass the level one test, either, even though I used computers a little when I was in school. A few of the professors even required everything to be word-processed. If it hadn't been for that, I would still be using a pencil for everything. We're lucky that our principal is even worse than we are about using computers. She refuses to even turn one on, let alone use one."

"I asked Sue Leonard, the union rep, if the administration could force us to take the test, and she said she'd look into it. However, she didn't seem very pleased with my asking, especially since she is the technology coordinator for the school," responded Mildred. "But she doesn't realize that some of us went to colleges that didn't have much in the way of computers. My college was nearly all minority kids, and it was very poor; we didn't have a lot of the equipment that most teacher education students have access to. My roommates and I shared one typewriter, and that was only ten years ago!"

"Well, we've missed the deadline to sign up for the class at the community college, so we'll have to figure something else out," said Rodney. "When did Sue say she'd have an answer for you?"

Discussion Points

1. What are some of the reasons why this teaching team has a problem with the use of computers?

2. Why have some teachers been able to adopt the use of technology much more quickly than others?

3. In addition to problems of computer use and technology, what are some of the other educational issues involved in this case?

4. Middle school teams often have one or two people who are more proficient in the use of technology than other team members, which poses a problem. How might interdisciplinary teams overcome this obstacle?

References

Ackerman, D. B. (1989). Intellectual and practical criteria for successful curriculum integration. In H. Hayes Jacobs (Ed.), *Interdisciplinary curriculum: Design and implementation* (pp. 25–38). Alexandria, VA: Association for Supervision and Curriculum Development.

Erb, T. O., & Doda, N. M. (1989). *Team organization: Promise, practices and possibilities.* Washington, DC: National Education Association.

Kellough, R. D., & Kellough, N. G. (1996). *Middle school teaching: A guide to methods and resources* (2nd ed.). Englewood Cliffs, NJ: Prentice Hall.

Stevenson, C. (1992). *Teaching ten to fourteen year olds.* New York: Longman.

Zessoules, R., & Gardner, H. (1991). Authentic assessment: Beyond the buzzword and into the classroom. In V. Perrone (Ed.), *Expanding student assessment* (pp. 47–71). Alexandria, VA: Association for Supervision and Curriculum Development.

❧ 5 ❧

ADMINISTRATION

The Case of the Uncooperative Faculty
The Case of the Fundamentalist Parent
The Case of the Bell-Crazed Faculty

ADMINISTRATION OF a middle school is no easier, though no more difficult, than administration of other types of schools. Yet in many school districts, middle schools are the institutions that are embarking on the most significant changes and innovations. As the educational culture cycles through new administrative procedures and philosophies, middle school principals often quietly make great strides in bringing about reform and change (George & Anderson, 1989). The "middle school philosophy" encompasses a wide range of educational innovations, from fundamental alterations to minor changes. Among the most important of these are leadership teams, interdisciplinary teams, advisory programs, and thematic units. Less significant changes include an improved flexible **block schedule** and prevocational or **exploratory programs**.

The middle school administrator must also deal with several publics, all of whom have large stakes in the success of the school. Parents have obvious stakes in school success, and the net of other stakeholders has widened in recent years. Businesses, particularly those involved in real estate and development, often use school success or reputation of success as selling points. Other industries, including governments, need to employ well-educated and well-trained individuals. The various media, too, often view information on education and schooling in a community as newsworthy. Special-interest groups, including religious ones, frequently use the schools as platforms from which to suggest the need for societal change.

Resistance to changes, whether major or minor, can take many forms: passive resistance, as teachers and others remain slow to accept new ways of teaching, or opposition that is active, vocal, and public. Regardless of the form, resistance should not be used as an excuse or as a way to disguise problems with implementation. All individuals involved in the process of change grow through stages of acceptance, commitment, and improvement. In middle schools, it is not uncommon to find individuals or groups of teachers who are uncomfortable with change, regardless of form or type, including the use of interdisciplinary teams (Murphy, 1991). Other programs—particularly the more difficult ones to implement, such as advisory programs and heterogeneous grouping—are often more difficult to implement, as the experiential learning curve is longer and steeper.

Faced with uncertainty and potential resistance from a variety of sources, middle school administrators must possess strong leadership skills. In addition, they must be able to effectively explain practices and organizations in a straightforward and knowledgeable manner; they must know middle schools and their practices, students, and teachers very well indeed (Lipsitz, 1984).

Special-interest groups have begun to emerge as robust critics of education and educational practices. Middle school administrators usually bear the brunt of such criticism. Here again, knowledge of educational research and effective communication and public relations skills are important. Wise principals, assistant principals, and teachers know that special-interest groups have the right to question what happens in schools, and they use engaging and knowledgeable responses to help educate them. This is not an easy task, especially when groups and organizations from outside the district become involved (Ledell & Arnsparger, 1993).

❧ ❧

The Case of the Uncooperative Faculty

The faculty of Lincoln Middle School was organized into interdisciplinary teams that appeared to be functioning very well after only two years. The school housed nearly six hundred sixth- through eighth-grade students, and since the move to interdisciplinary teams, both school climate and academic achievement had improved.

The school also used a form of core integrated curriculum within all of the teams. The teams had participated in several in-service programs concerning curriculum and instruction before instituting attempts at integration. The daily schedule was built around flexible blocks, and teams determined their own academic and core schedules. Most teams used forms of heterogeneous grouping for instruction, and they enjoyed strong parent relations. A leadership team met every week with the principal. Although the principal held veto power for decisions, the group often convinced him to follow their wishes and plans for the school.

The final phase of implementing middle school practices included a limited biweekly **intramural program** and a daily period of advisor-advisee or teacher-based guidance. It was hoped that the advisor-advisee program would help Lincoln students make good decisions, establish more positive teacher-student relations, help students with study skills as they moved toward high school, and also help them make good decisions about sexual behavior.

Over the summer a group of Lincoln teachers had been paid to develop a set of materials for use in the advisor-advisee program. The result of their efforts was three grade-level sets of materials gleaned from a variety of sources, including programs of other schools, commercial products, and materials provided by the school counselor. The materials were organized into four major topical areas: life and study skills, interpersonal relationships, communication skills, and adolescent development. The activities and materials were designed to build in complexity through each grade level.

The summer group led a full-day faculty in-service program during the week before school started. First, the counselor presented a rationale for advisor-advisee programs, and then each of the three grade-level groups presented its materials. The faculty appeared to be excited about the program and pleased that the materials were extensive enough to offset their concern over preparation time. The school calendar was blocked out into the four topic areas, and a general schedule of weekly topics was also provided. The new program was to begin the second day of school, and would take place for thirty minutes at the beginning of each day.

During the first few weeks, the program appeared to be successful; the introductory letters sent to parents were received well, and the students seemed to be enjoying their assigned tasks. The tasks were mostly paper-and-pencil worksheets, designed to provoke discussion, thought, value development, and skill improvement. No grades were given, but the evaluation for reporting purposes would include "satisfactory" or "unsatisfactory" notations.

Problems began to occur during the sixth week of the program: the students became bored with the worksheets, and discipline and order problems during the advisory period increased. The teachers, though happy with the materials, found that the concepts and content were difficult to communicate, and the personal nature of some of the topics and activities was threatening to some. Most of the teachers found it difficult to talk about such things as secondary sexual characteristics, sexual behavior, emotions, child-parent relationships, peer pressure, and other sensitive topics.

To minimize their discomfort, most of the teachers added more worksheets and instituted "study time," "free reading," and "homework catch-up" as part of the daily program. Indeed, in many teams, the daily period deteriorated into student chatting and general free time. By Thanksgiving, several parents had called to express their displeasure with the program.

During the last faculty meeting before the winter holiday break, the principal stated his concerns about the program and said that after the break he would begin systematic and unannounced observations during the advisor-advisee period. He felt that his observing the teachers would prompt them to work at getting the program back on track. Several teachers complained about this plan and voiced their own concerns about the advisor-advisee program. Some suggested that the program be scrapped after break and redesigned for next year. However, the principal refused to accept this idea. Instead, he encouraged the teachers to spend a little more time on the planning and execution of the program.

After the winter holidays, the principal met with each team to discuss the advisor-advisee program and then began to observe the classes. His postobservation conferences were heated and emotional, as teachers vented their frustrations and anger about the program. Many of them, including two entire interdisciplinary teams, refused to cooperate and began to use the period for additional academic teaching.

By mid-March, little was left of the advisor-advisee program. The area on the report card was left blank during the fourth six-week grading period, and it was obvious that the principal was upset and angry over the situation. He refused to discuss the program with anyone and after March discontinued his first-period observations. As the year began to close, the teams and teachers not-so-secretly wished for an end of the program, and were concerned and afraid of what might happen next year.

Discussion Points

1. Why didn't the principal's strategy of observing the advisory program work?
2. The process Lincoln went through to develop its advisory program is typical, and so are the difficulties the school experienced. What are the major causes of the problems?
3. As the school year ends, what options are available to Lincoln concerning its advisor-advisee program?
4. Which option do you think has the best chance for success, and why?

The Case of the Fundamentalist Parent

Riverview County was a great place to live. There was little crime in this community of nearly a hundred thousand people, and the county's economy was fueled by a stable industry of several computer companies, agriculture, and some summer tourism. The schools had been managed by conservative elected school boards for many years. Most of the elementary and high schools in the district took a fairly traditional approach to instruction and curriculum, but the four middle schools had been slowly moving from junior high to middle school structures for several years. All the middle schools had interdisciplinary teams, heterogeneous grouping for most instruction, well-designed and effective advisory programs, and many exploratory and prevocational programs. The schools all had strong **interscholastic athletics**, and in addition to playing against the other schools in the district, the teams played against other middle school teams from up to sixty miles away.

Each of the schools had strong parent groups, but the group at Patterson Middle School seemed to be the most consistently active. Patterson boasted a large group of parent volunteers who were involved with some of the teams in developing thematic units as well as other instructional activities. The school counselor, Judy Pitts, coordinated the volunteers and also—along with the principal, Deborah Quigley, and two other teachers—held tutoring training sessions for parent volunteers several times throughout the year. During one of the February training sessions some concerns began to emerge.

The sessions consisted of four short workshops that covered most of the developmental characteristics of middle school students, including some materials about how middle schoolers learn best. Also included were brief segments about questioning skills, higher order thinking, and assessing learning. Judy and Dr. Quigley had become very comfortable with conducting the sessions and had also become friends with several of the volunteers.

The February session was focused on higher order thinking and problem solving. One parent, Robert Wilson, the father of a sixth-grade student, became quite agitated when he was confronted with the idea that some problems can have several viable solutions and that students are often capable of generating effective and creative solutions themselves. Throughout the session, Mr. Wilson adamantly and loudly expressed his opposition to this type of teaching, stating that such thinking was anti-Christian and caused children to question the authority of their parents and the church. The session broke down into a free-for-all, "teacher bashing" discussion that left the two presenters feeling terrible.

By March Mr. Wilson had visited the school several times to speak with Dr. Quigley, had called on the superintendent, and had made telephone calls to each of the board members. He also had gathered support from some other parents and had begun to systematically question nearly all of his daughter's assignments. He was particularly concerned about the advisory program, which included sections on substance abuse, growth and development, and career exploration, as well as family planning, AIDS, and sexual behavior. The focus of these sections was clearly on sexual abstinence, sound decision making, and skills for dealing with peer pressures. Mr. Wilson thought that none of these materials should be taught or used in schools. He believed that the school's "opt out" procedure should be changed to an "opt in" format, so that parents would have to choose the program rather than having to decide not to participate.

As the situation became more and more contentious, the volunteer program began to deteriorate. For the first time since its inception, volunteer parents were calling in sick or simply calling to inform Judy that they would no longer be coming to the school. The teachers who relied on the volunteers also became involved as they felt the pressures of having to regroup and reassign students. The teachers also began to discuss many of the issues that Mr. Wilson was bringing up. Many of the teachers who lived in this very conservative community strongly supported many of Mr. Wilson's positions.

Mr. Wilson now questioned many of the school's practices besides the advisory program. He wrote letters to Dr. Quigley (with copies to the school board and the superintendent) asking for specific reasons why the school was divided into teams, why the teams used interdisciplinary thematic units, why the special education students were "included" with the regular classes, why the Pledge of Allegiance was not said daily, and why prevocational and exploratory classes formed part of the schoolday. He also appeared to have access to several organizations that provided him with statistics and research that supported his positions. All of his meetings with Dr. Quigley and her staff were cordial and polite, though tense. But the meetings went nowhere. Mr. Wilson would simply thank the principal and teachers and leave, usually before they had had a chance either to ask questions of him or to discuss the issues.

Dr. Quigley had a very good professional reputation in the district, but the barrage of attacks on her school was beginning to take its toll. The two local television stations interviewed her, and the newspaper began a series about "innovation in education" that appeared to be heavily slanted toward a "back to basics" philosophy. Now, as she sat looking at the day's mail, she saw the board of education meeting agenda: item number four was "Public Comment" and had Robert Wilson's name beside it. Suddenly, she felt very much alone and afraid.

Discussion Points

1. What are some of the issues involved in this complex case?
2. How should the principal prepare to address the problem of the upcoming board of education meeting?
3. Would you agree or disagree with the statement that parents always have the right to question what schools do with their children? Why or why not?
4. What characteristics should middle school leaders have in order to manage good middle schools, keeping in mind the extent to which the middle school movement differs from traditional approaches?

The Case of the Bell-Crazed Faculty

The principal of Greentown Middle School, Ann Melrose, was slowly transforming a junior high school into a middle school. Her first step was to set up interdisciplinary teams. Only after a year of getting accustomed to teaming did she begin to implement some other parts of the "middle school philosophy." Elements such as advisory groups, exploratory and prevocational programs, heterogeneous grouping, and curriculum changes were scheduled to take place over the next five years. This fall, after much discussion with her teachers, she developed a flexible block schedule that allowed the school's seven teams to control all aspects of the instructional day except for exploratory times and lunch. Ms. Melrose gave the teachers their respective teams' schedules on the first workday of the new school year, and at first they seemed excited and enthusiastic about the schedule. Several of the teams had already begun planning thematic units for later in the year, and it appeared that the new schedule would help them manage the units more efficiently.

The first indications of trouble came as the principal began to roam the halls during the second week of school. The problems seemed to come during breaks between classes, when large numbers of students were in the halls, getting books and bookbags from their lockers, talking, laughing, and doing what most middle school students do between classes—letting off some energy. The leadership team had agreed that four minutes was enough time for students to change classes, since that was how long class changes had taken last year, when there were bells to mark the end and beginning of class periods. As Ms. Melrose wandered the halls, she began to note how long the students were taking to complete their book exchange and get back into the rooms. In most cases, it was nearly seven minutes before all the students were settled; in a couple of cases, nearly nine minutes passed.

The principal's first attempt at solving the problem didn't seem to help. She wrote a memo to all faculty asking that at least one member of each team be in the halls to monitor student movement during each class change. She checked to see if the teachers were complying with her request, and in most cases a teacher from the team was in the hall, trying to get the students to move quickly to the next class. However, the time taken changed very little. The next time she checked, there were no nine-minute changes, but most were still taking between five and seven minutes, even with the teachers' attempts to speed things up.

Other problems began to occur as well. Until now, the school had not been known for rowdy students, fighting, or other disruptive behaviors. But now, during one week there were three fistfights in the eighth-grade hall, and all began during class changes.

The principal's next memo was worded a little more strongly, suggesting that the teachers take some time to explain the importance of quick class changes to the students, and that perhaps more than one teacher should be in the halls during class changes. She also suggested that since each team was responsible for its own academic subject schedule, maybe the teams should rework the schedules so that no two teams' students changed classes at the same time. There were three sixth-grade teams, two seventh-grade, and two eighth-grade, and Ms. Melrose felt that the team leaders could easily get together and arrange for schedules that didn't overlap.

The schedule was the Penguin Team's major topic of discussion in that day's team meeting. All four of the seventh-grade Penguin teachers were clearly upset at not only the content of the principal's memo but also its tone.

"I think we should go back to the bell schedule we had last year," suggested Joann Wiggins, the team's science teacher. "I like the extra time for labs, but this is ridiculous."

"Well, if she had asked any of us about this flexible schedule, she would have found out that we really don't see much of a need for it," added Jeanette Lefevre. Jeanette was the team leader and taught its math classes, including two sections of pre-algebra. "I've been teaching seventh-grade math for a long time, and I've got it pretty well worked out, even with all of the extracurricular interruptions we have to put up with. Do you want me to go to her?"

"The Shark Team basically uses the same schedule we do. We even go to lunch the same time. How can we both change our schedules so we are never in the hall at the same time? That would mean chopping the schedule up even further. No, I say we ask Richard and see if the Sharks want to go to her as well. Maybe if we both approach her at the same time. . . . " Joann stopped for a second and then continued, "And what about the sixth grade? There are three sixth-grade teams! I'll bet Susan is fit to be tied. She had a cow last year just going to teams!"

The rest of the team chuckled for a moment, and then Dewayne Green, the language arts teacher, spoke up. "Well, I think we should give it a try. I really like this block schedule stuff, and we've only been doing it for a few weeks. Besides, I really haven't been pulling my share of hall duty during the breaks, and I think if we just kind of watch a little more carefully, we can solve this problem."

At that point, the meeting broke into two different conversations. Just as Jeanette was about to pull the team back together, the classroom door opened and Susan Macintosh, one of the sixth-grade team leaders, leaned in the doorway and said, "Come on, guys, we're on our way to see Ann about this memo. Do you want to come?" They could see three other teachers in the hall waiting for Susan.

Discussion Points

1. What seems to be the primary issue, or issues, in this case?
2. Is the principal's request for the teams to change their schedules a reasonable one? Why or why not?

3. The Penguin Team seems aware of some of the advantages of block schedules. What could the principal do to help them recognize some of the more subtle, but powerful, advantages?

4. How could the teams and team leaders help solve the problem?

References

George, P., & Anderson, W. G. (1989). Maintaining the middle school: A national survey. *NASSP Bulletin, 73,* 86–94.

Ledell, M., & Arnsparger, A. (1993). *How to deal with community criticism of school change.* Alexandria, VA: Association for Supervision and Curriculum Development.

Lipsitz, J. (1984). *Successful schools for young adolescents.* New Brunswick, NJ: Transaction Books.

Murphy, J. (1991). *Restructuring schools: Capturing and assessing the phenomena.* New York: Teachers College Press.

❧ 6 ❧

EXPLORATORY AND INTRAMURAL PROGRAMS

The Case of the Overburdened Exploratory Team
The Case of the Surprise Budget Cuts
The Case of the Stretched Intramurals

THE PURPOSES OF EXPLORATORY and intramural programs and activities in a middle school are closely related to both the physical and intellectual development of the child. Most middle school students are beginning to display curiosity about careers and their future as they grow from egocentric views to more empathetic ones (Schurr, Thomason & Thompson, 1995). They are intensely interested in making sense of the world. In addition, they are often beginning to engage in creative activities at a heightened level of interest and skill. Exploratory programs introduce students to a variety of careers and interests (Toepfer, 1994). They represent a departure from the traditional "shop" or "home ec" classes, allowing students to pursue and investigate a wide range of topics (Messick & Reynolds, 1992). Exploratory classes include but are not limited to:

- art
- creative writing

- vocal and instrumental music
- dance
- drama and theater arts
- media arts and multimedia production
- television production
- foreign languages
- health and growth education
- physical education and fitness
- home economics, home arts, and life management
- environmental education and ecological studies
- business and marketing
- computers and technology education
- technology, technical skill development, and unified arts

The length of exploratory courses or classes varies according to school and district schedules, and the number and types of courses are often related to financial constraints and budgetary considerations. Courses generally last from six to nine weeks, and students typically are given choices throughout the year. Unfortunately, the nature of some of the exploratory courses may limit students' opportunities; for example, students who choose band as an elective or exploratory usually remain in the band through their middle school years, a commitment that may prevent them from exploring other options.

Intramural sports or other club opportunities are often large parts of a middle school organization and schedule. The focus is on participation and learning, rather than competition and scores. In some schools, intramurals are designed and implemented by regular classroom teachers who offer a range of activities for short periods of time.

Exploratory teachers may be placed on one of the interdisciplinary teams, or they may be organized as either a team or a department (Kellough & Kellough, 1996). Exploratory teams usually consist of groups of teachers who specialize in such educational program areas as business and marketing, domestic arts, technology or industrial applications, vocal music, band or orchestra, or drama and performing arts. In many cases these teachers have had significant additional training in these areas as well as having completed traditional teacher education programs. The arrangements and organizational patterns for exploratory teachers pose interesting problems and challenges for middle schools. For example, it is often extremely difficult to arrange a schedule that allows exploratory teachers to have the same planning periods as core interdisciplinary teams, since team teachers' planning times are generally scheduled during the periods when their students are with the exploratory teachers. Therefore, communication and planning coordination are difficult to achieve even when exploratory teachers are members of a team. Exploratory teachers, however, are integral to the effectiveness of middle schools. Team leaders of exemplary schools often plan for extra meetings and work out methods of communicating with exploratory teachers.

The Case of the Overburdened Exploratory Team

Benjamin Franklin Middle School was considered the best in the city, and visitors from surrounding states were seen in the school almost daily. The principal, Joyce Waters, was highly respected and was often the keynote speaker at education conferences. The student population was fairly large, more than six hundred, but the interdisciplinary teams and "house" arrangement allowed the students and faculty to feel as if they were part of small families linked for a common purpose. The school had pioneered middle school practices more than twelve years ago, and although the transition had been bumpy at times, the school had grown and learned from mistakes, so that it was now considered exemplary in nearly every respect. There were interdisciplinary teams in all grades; the curriculum had been designed and redesigned to accommodate interdisciplinary themes, differentiated learning styles, and handicapping conditions; and the school's intramural and exploratory programs had won several awards. The main building, which dated from the late 1960s, appeared fresh and well maintained; several smaller buildings, including the newest "exploratory wing," had been added over the last several years.

The exploratory team consisted of four teachers who had worked together for ten years. Each was also assigned to one of the grade-level teams, and they worked hard to ensure that their curriculum and programs complemented and supported those of the grade-level teams. The exploratory curriculum consisted of three overlapping and complementary program areas: industrial arts, domestic arts, and business and marketing. Mike Taylor's industrial arts program offered students an opportunity to explore typical industrial careers and also was a key link to the high school's "tech prep" program. The domestic arts program, led by Susan Albright, combined traditional curriculum areas with some high-tech applications, such as computerized budgeting and menu development and microprocessor-managed energy control. It also touched on several technical aspects of the medical profession. Angela Lemon's business and marketing program focused on the technical aspects of retailing, marketing, and business management, and students were often placed in businesses as "interns." All students, including the sixth-graders, were scheduled for nine-week programs in two of the three areas each year.

The other "noncore" areas were art, vocal music, and band, which rotated with the exploratory programs and allowed all students to have the widest possible set of choices throughout their three years at Franklin. This arrangement also allowed the class sizes to be a bit smaller; class sizes for all the exploratory programs except band averaged around eighteen to twenty students.

Franklin Middle School housed, as part of its student body, one class of about twenty students who were emotionally and behaviorally disturbed. Most of these students had been through the court system for crimes ranging from vandalism to assault with deadly weapons. Most were assigned to a grade-level team, but due to their unpredictable and often violent behavior, only a few actually had classes with their respective teams. Twelve of these students were regularly scheduled into exploratory classes. Their Individualized Education Plans (IEPs) included their academic and behavioral objectives, and in nearly all the cases the inclusion of the exploratory classes had been decided without any input from the exploratory teachers. In the past, the exploratory teachers had been happy to include the troubled students and had worked closely with the special education teachers and the regular classroom teachers to make sure these students had positive and rewarding experiences. During the last two years, the number of such students had risen from two or three per year to twelve or more, of varying ages and achievement. These students were present in nearly every class period of the day for the exploratory team.

"They're neat kids, but they're driving us all nuts! I have to watch them every minute of the class, and although they haven't been violent in class, we all know about some of the things they've done, so I'm always on my toes. Sometimes they scare me. I'm also scared to refer any of them for internships. They never sit still, they can't listen, and getting any work out of them is next to impossible. Some days I don't think I'm doing them any good at all. And I think the rest of the kids are suffering, too, and some of them seem scared as well." Angela ran her fingers through her hair and shook her head as she spoke.

"John's the worst in my room—I have some potentially dangerous equipment in there and I worry that he might hurt himself or someone else." Mike lounged across an old tattered couch, his hands linked behind his head.

"My equipment isn't dangerous, but it's expensive, and most of them can't seem to do anything gently," said Angela. "I know they've got it rough, and I feel sorry for them. Our classes are the only 'normal' classes they have all day. They stay cooped up in that classroom, and they don't even eat with the other kids."

"What if we put them all together? I think I could handle them better if they were all there at once. At least the other kids wouldn't suffer," Susan suggested.

"I doubt whether the schedule would work, and the point is to have them with other kids, isn't it? My problem is with the ones who truly have attention deficit disorders. They really try sometimes, but they don't have the ability to attend for very long. That stuff the consultant told us to try didn't work—those techniques might work in a regular classroom. If I didn't have anybody else in the room, I could do it, but there are twenty other kids in there!" As Mike spoke, he headed for the door. "I think I'll talk to Joyce again. We need some help."

"I don't remember a year when I've been so tired at the end of the day," Susan said, "and I know it's because of these kids. But I also realize that given their histories, they're really doing pretty well. At least we know they are interested and having some fun in our classes. And they do seem to be learning, even though it's hard to tell that sometimes."

"I know, Susan. I really haven't had a lot of trouble with them—it's just that they are so, well, active. But we haven't had the kind of trouble the regular classroom teachers have had. Remember what John did last year? I don't think I could handle that kind of violence in my classroom."

Discussion Points

1. What are the problem areas in this case, and whose problems are they?
2. What options are available to the exploratory team?
3. If the options are limited, how do you suggest the team members go about dealing with the troubled students in their classes?
4. Who else should become part of the solution to this problem? Why?
5. Do you think this problem is more typical of middle schools than of elementary or high schools? Why?

❧ ❧

The Case of the Surprise Budget Cuts

Martin Luther King, Jr., Middle School was located in the heart of a large metropolitan area. The school was surrounded by many boarded-up storefronts, along with a few small shops and retail outlets. Just to the west of the school, an empty public housing project stood as a silent reminder of the neighborhood's deterioration. It was known that drugs were bought and sold openly in many of the doorways and street corners, and several shootings had taken place on nearby streets since the school year began.

Martin Luther King School was a source of pride and hope for many in this troubled community. For the past ten years the school had provided a safe and caring environment for its nine hundred students, and the teachers who made up the interdisciplinary teams in the school were known for their advocacy on behalf of students and the school. Most of the teachers at King had asked to teach in this school, and turnover was lower than the district average. The principal, Mark Wilson, had grown up in the neighborhood, knew most of the students by name, and—knowing how difficult it was to raise children in this environment—treated parents with respect and dignity. His parent involvement program was envied by other principals who had problems getting parents to attend conferences. Mr. Wilson's parent leadership team ran a school store, volunteered in many classes, and taught several of the intramural offerings. Most of the school and community functions were extremely well attended by teachers, students, and parents. Academically, the students at King scored just above the district average and near the state average, an accomplishment that had taken Mr. Wilson and his staff nearly a decade to reach. Since he had become principal, student suspensions had decreased dramatically, and minor discipline problems were generally dealt with on the respective teams.

Central to King's successes were the extracurricular, exploratory, intramural, and interscholastic sports programs. Students were not allowed to try out for any interscholastic team unless they were passing all of their classes, and the school gymnasium was open until very late each night with girls' and boys' basketball and volleyball practices. The intramural program took place during alternating six-week periods during the schoolday, which was extended by forty-five minutes to allow for the programs. Several parents and other volunteers added staffing to this popular program, which offered a wide range of topics and activities. The choices ranged from short courses in computers to chess and modeling clubs, and from aerobic exercise to the study of oil painting and foreign languages.

The school's exploratory program had a limited budget, but it managed to offer band, art, vocal music, drama and theater, business and marketing, data processing and electronic arts, home arts and cooking, and television production. Full-time teachers were assigned to band, art, business, data processing, and home arts. These positions were state funded, and all five teachers had been at King for many years. Vocal music and drama were both taught by one teacher, whose salary was paid through a federal program that targeted at-risk students. Another full-time teacher taught television production, a position funded through an ongoing grant from a consortium of television and radio stations in the city.

The exploratory program was immensely successful. King students had performed in concerts around the state, had their artwork shown in local and state galleries, and competed well in interstate business contests, once beating a collegiate team in a stock market game. Annually, students produced a documentary of school life, some of which had been shown on local television stations, including the local public broadcasting station. Students from the three feeder elementary schools often vied for placement on the waiting lists for their favored exploratory program.

But this year the exploratory team was worried. The economy was in a slump, and there were rumors that the business consortium was going to reduce or eliminate funding for the television production exploratory program. The district had given its teachers a long overdue raise that was proving to be a greater burden on the budget than anticipated. The board of education had recently passed a ruling that class sizes in the primary grades had to be reduced, and since no additional teachers were hired, this meant that class sizes in the middle and high schools rose accordingly.

On a warm August day just before the school year began, the team's worst fears came to pass. The principal gathered the seven members of the exploratory team together in his office for a meeting. He began by saying, "It's pretty bad news, folks. I just left the superintendent's office, and I don't know any other way than to tell this to you straight out. I want you to know, though, that I fought as hard as I could, and I will keep fighting until we see this thing through."

Mr. Wilson cleared his throat, sat down behind his cluttered desk, and continued, "There is going to be an across-the-board budget cut of 15 percent for everyone, including the regular classroom teachers. Second, we will lose two full-time regular classroom teachers, most likely in the seventh and eighth grades, since the numbers for the sixth grade are pretty high. Third, there will be no funds for vocal music or drama. Fourth . . . "

"Wait a minute, Mr. Wilson," interrupted Jeremy Pines, the music and drama teacher. "Do you mean to tell me that I don't have a job?" Jeremy stood up and began to pace around the cluttered office.

"Hold on, Jeremy, let me finish," responded the principal. "Nobody is out of a job, at least not yet. Let's see, where was I? Oh yes, fourth, business and marketing programs at the middle school have been cut by 50 percent." Trisha Fellows, the business teacher, sucked in her breath audibly, as Mr. Wilson continued. "Fifth, the consortium is cutting its funding to the school by 75 percent. Last year, they gave us nearly sixty thousand dollars, and this year they are giving us fifteen." He leaned forward in his chair. "Now let me remind you, I'm telling you this right now so the rumor mill doesn't make things look worse than they are. I just now got out of the meeting, and I came to you first."

Rachel Stein, the data-processing teacher, stood up and said, "Mark, this is too much. If I calculate this correctly, we are not losing one, but two and a half positions from our team alone! How can they do this? After all we've done for this school and this school district, how can they do this to us? Are the other middle schools getting hit like this?"

"In fact, they are getting hit worse than we are. Kennedy is losing a total of seven teachers, and Burbank is losing six," answered Mr. Wilson. "But before we go off and do something silly, let's try to figure out how we can absorb some of these cuts." He opened a manila file folder and handed each teacher a sheet of paper. "Now look at this. I think we may be able to solve this problem. These are just a few ideas that I scribbled down when the boss was unloading all of this on us."

Discussion Points

1. The funding problems seem insoluble, yet the principal seems to have some ideas about how to solve them. What might these ideas be?
2. What kinds of strategies should the teachers follow in this situation?
3. What other resources are available to the staff at King, and how could they be used?
4. How should the principal and teachers go about informing the rest of the staff about the problem?

The Case of the Stretched Intramurals

The intramural program at Gardner Middle School was a relatively new addition. The school was located in a working-class suburban neighborhood, and its students came from a wide variety of economic, social, and cultural backgrounds. For the last four years, the seven-hundred-student school had been organized into interdisciplinary teams. It was governed by a leadership team of teachers, parents, and the principal, and its teachers had implemented several integrated thematic curriculum units that had proven effective as well as innovative. The school's advisory program had begun a year ago. Although there had been a few difficulties, the wrinkles seemed to have been ironed out, and this year the program was working smoothly. The committee that had designed the intramural program had felt that the program would benefit from testing, so it had recommended that the school operate the intramurals on a bimonthly basis for the first year. Therefore, the programs, activities, classes, and mini-courses would be offered during September, November, January, March, and May.

Near the end of the previous year, the committee had surveyed the staff and collected a long list of hobbies, interests, athletics and sports, and ideas for social club sponsorships. The committee had then contacted each staff person and asked for preferences and additional ideas. Each faculty member had been asked to design a flyer that "advertised" his or her intramural offering, and these flyers had been distributed and displayed around the school toward the end of the year. Rising seventh- and eighth-grade students had been given a ballot upon which they were to enter their choices for next fall's intramural activities. Sixth-graders would have to choose in the fall when they arrived at Gardner, but when the committee had counted the ballots and organized the schedule, it had reserved some slots for the sixth-grade students. Given the nature of some of the offerings, the committee had been unable to give every student his or her first choice of activities, but in most cases students had been granted their first or second choice. The committee had assured the students that over the course of the year, they would have more opportunities to sign up for their preferred activity.

Intramurals took place at the end of each schoolday, and for the first week, the program seemed to be doing well. Midway through the second week, however, five team leaders requested a meeting with the principal, Dolores Martinez.

"Ms. Martinez, this intramural schedule is going to be too much for us," said Alicia Hatfield. "We aren't even through the second week, and my team is going nuts with this. We have sixth-, seventh-, and eighth-graders in the same room, and I don't know how it happened, but Susan has twenty kids in there all doing tie-dyeing in her science room. It's a mess."

"Yeah, and Steven doesn't even have enough chairs in his room," interrupted another team leader, Grace McDonald.

"Wait a minute, folks," said Ms. Martinez, "Hold on! I want to listen to what all of you have to say about this, but I can't do it if you're all talking at once. You're picking up bad habits from your students. Okay, let's start with the numbers issue. How did so many kids get scheduled into those classes? There was supposed to be a limit on all the classes, including the sports. How could so many kids have signed up?"

"We're not sure," admitted Alicia. "I think the numbers are probably okay for most of the classes, but having three grade levels in the same room is tough, too. My sixth-graders are scared to death of the eighth-graders, and I don't know all their names, and they lie about whose room they're in or what team they're on."

"Hold on, wait a minute. You're talking about a bunch of problems here. Why weren't these problems brought up before we started this thing?" asked Ms. Martinez. "I walked around the building yesterday during intramurals, and I thought things were going very smoothly. I was surprised at how calm everyone was. It was a little noisy here and there, but for the most part, the noise was good noise. You know, kids doing things and feeling happy about it."

"Well, the honeymoon is over," responded Jim Nelson, another team leader. "I say we put a moratorium on intramurals until we get a handle on things. Most of us don't have time to plan our next activity, anyway."

"Let's not be too hasty," answered Ms. Martinez. "I'll put it on the agenda for next week's faculty meeting. In fact, that's the only thing I'll put on the agenda. Until then, let's try to sort things out and keep a lid on the situation. The kids are having a good time, but if it's as bad as you all say, we'll need to make some changes."

Discussion Points

1. How would you define the problems that are arising in the intramural program?
2. The principal does not seem quite as upset as the team leaders. What does her reaction say about school communications?
3. What are some alternative solutions to the problems?
4. What role should the planning committee play in the process?

References

Kellough, R. D., & Kellough, N. G. (1996). *Middle school teaching: A guide to methods and resources.* Englewood Cliffs, NJ: Prentice Hall.

Messick, R., & Reynolds, K. (1992). *Middle level curriculum in action.* White Plains, NY: Longman.

Schurr, D. L., Thomason, J., & Thompson, M. (1995). Expanded exploratories, electives, and intramurals. In J. H. Lounsbury (Ed.), *Teaching at the middle level* (pp. 99–102). Lexington, MA: D. C. Heath.

Toepfer, C. F., Jr. (1994). Vocational/career/occupational education at the middle level: What is appropriate for young adolescents? *Middle School Journal, 25* (3), 59–65.

৯ 7 ৶

GOVERNANCE AND TEACHER LEADERSHIP

The Case of the Pushy Principal
The Case of the Combative Leadership Team
The Case of the Overly Successful Project

IT MAY SEEM UNUSUAL, even inappropriate, to discuss governance and leadership separately from administration (see chapter 5). But exemplary middle schools are often places where governance is shared and where teachers are truly leaders. Interdisciplinary teams, like schools, grow and become increasingly effective as they reflect the nature and character of the team's leaders. George and Alexander (1993, p. 497) are persuasive in their belief that the vision of effective middle school leadership comes from clear understanding of the young adolescent learner, sound and uniquely responsive planning and implementation, and the shared engagement and decision making of all the school's stakeholders. To this end, teams of teacher leaders, usually representative of the teams and the various other departments, can often be found working in concert with principals and parents toward responsive and constructive middle school programs. Indeed, it is not uncommon for middle school administrators to defer decisions

77

and program directions to a leadership team of professionals and parents.

Yet the notion of teacher leadership, with its requisite skills, attitudes, knowledge, and development, can be elusive. Fullan (1994) believes that a lack of proper perspective and conceptualization of the teacher leader is one reason why teacher leadership is not taken seriously. He suggests that all teachers, not simply a few, must undertake leadership roles if reform efforts are to succeed.

Middle schools should be noted for how seriously they take this challenge; the complex changes needed for a middle school to become effective and exemplary rely heavily on teachers embracing leadership roles. Leadership teams, interdisciplinary teams, advisory programs, integrated and thematic curricula, technology education, and effective scheduling count on the professional expertise of many individuals and their ability to communicate with and lead peers. For a school to be successful, teachers must forge the "educative communities" that Goodlad (1994) prescribes as necessary for public education to renew itself.

The processes, as well as the starting points, are different and removed from the traditional administrative model that remains characteristic of most other schools. The processes must begin with teacher education and development that includes leadership skills and knowledge. Coupled with this, there must be a commitment to the view of teachers as professionals in their own right, who must undertake leadership as one of their professional responsibilities. Effective middle school teachers who teach in exemplary schools recognize their roles as leaders and agents of change; in such schools groups of teachers, both as interdisciplinary teaching teams and governance teams, are frequently called upon to make decisions regarding the full range of school functions.

In spite of the importance of teacher leadership, institutions that educate future and practicing teachers rarely include leadership as a formal part of the curriculum. This lack leaves many teachers with little in the way of leadership skills and little understanding of its importance. Some individual teachers unfortunately remain strong in their belief that educational leadership is not part of their role. Such teachers are reluctant to champion those who advocate teacher leadership. In addition, many educational leaders and members of the public still view teaching as a relatively easy activity and tend to place educational leadership directly and solely in the hands of a few experts or managers.

Middle school leadership teams must deal with constraints, obstacles, and a variety of challenges. Faced with some strong administrators, leadership teams may become little more than distributors of information about decisions that have already been made. Leadership teams that lack strong internal leadership or group skills may become dysfunctional and have serious difficulties reaching decisions. Political implications, petty jealousies, and personal conflicts may subvert and damage improvement or management efforts by leadership teams. Nonetheless, middle school leadership teams can and do manage to operate effectively.

The Case of the Pushy Principal

The halls at Kennedy Middle School looked more like those of an elementary school than those of a middle school. Team pictures and cutouts were hung on nearly every available surface. Students' names were neatly printed on profiles in one section of the entryway wall, and students' work could be seen throughout the building. Signs and posters with proverbs and famous quotations were hung on each classroom and entry doorway. The bright blue lockers were similarly decorated, though the art was obviously student work. A visitor would have no doubt as to the name of any team that was housed in any section of the building.

The building itself was far from new, but showed evidence of recent exterior remodeling and painting. The interior, however, had been transformed. Until this school year, Kennedy Middle School had been Kennedy Junior High School. It had operated much like a high school in miniature, with academic departments, a rigid eight-period schoolday, and interscholastic sports teams. The teachers had rarely worked together outside of strict department functions. This year, the school was staffed and organized in interdisciplinary teams. It operated without bells on a flexible seven-period schedule, operated a teacher advisory program, offered intramural rather than interscholastic sports, featured a fully staffed exploratory and prevocational program, and had a new leadership structure.

Gary Greenberg, the new principal of Kennedy, was proud of his achievements, especially considering his hard-fought battles for additional budget resources, staff development, and parent support. He and his leadership team had transformed the junior high into a fully operational middle school in six short months. Now, three months into the school year, everything appeared to be going smoothly. The holidays were nearing, and although the incidence of problem student behavior was higher than normal, the principal felt satisfied.

Before starting his new job, Mr. Greenberg, a high school principal, had attended several workshops about middle schools. He was sold on the concept of a developmentally responsive school for preadolescent students. He had garnered support from a small cadre of parents and central office administrators, and his faculty, though initially hesitant to make such sweeping changes, appeared supportive. The principal was the school's biggest booster, often speaking to community groups about the changes at Kennedy.

Monday's faculty meeting, however, had not gone as he had expected. When he had told the faculty that he expected each team to implement one thematic integrated unit before the end of the year, several teachers had voiced strong opposition, suggesting that the school was moving too quickly. Then, when he had added that he expected each team to spend at least thirty minutes of the team planning period discussing students, several others had stated that they were already spending nearly all their planning time talking about students and student behavior. When he had suggested home visits so that teachers could view firsthand the homes from which the students came, one teacher, Stephanie Peters, had refused outright.

Today's leadership team meeting was not going well, either. Mr. Greenberg approached the subject of Monday's meeting carefully, stating that he did not plan on operating the school without full staff support. He also apologized for "coming on too strong" during the full faculty meeting and said he wanted to hear from the team leaders before making any more suggestions.

"Well, Gary, it's been a tough year. Everybody's a little stressed with the holidays coming up, the kids are getting pretty restless, and it doesn't seem like we're covering as much material as we used to," Ruby Snyder, one of the seventh-grade team leaders said. "This team business is great, but it takes time to make it work. And I have the feeling that some of the teams aren't getting along too well."

"Which ones? There are things we can do to help teams get along, and I want to help," the principal replied.

"Well, I wouldn't go so far as to say 'not getting along,' Gary, but as Ruby said, it takes time for things to, you know, gel," said Sam Arnold. Sam was a sixth-grade team leader who was known for his close ties with parents and the community. "We're just getting settled into a nice schedule, and this thematic unit will throw things into a tailspin. Why this year?"

"Sam, remember when you visited the school at Long Point? They did five or six thematic units a year, and they got a lot of support from the community for their efforts, and the teachers seemed to love them," the principal replied.

"It's still a lot," interjected Millie Thomas, the school guidance counselor. "Right now the teachers are just trying to survive until the holidays. I know you're seeing a lot more students in the office, and that's just a symptom. Everyone's uptight, and adding to the burden will just make it worse."

"I don't think so. One of the primary reasons for moving to interdisciplinary teams was to allow more integration of the curriculum. Now that the teams are in place, I'd like to try it. It's possible that some new activities and interests might alleviate some of the behavior problems. What could I do to help the teams get moving on this?"

"Well, it might help if you'd back off on the home visits—you know, let that ride while we work on the curriculum. Maybe get to it next year," Ruby suggested.

"That's another big piece of getting the students back on track, though," replied Mr. Greenberg. "It's not so bad. I try to talk to parents each time I take a kid home, and I think it helps. You know, a lot of our parents aren't real fond of school. Many of them never got past the eighth grade, and school isn't a pleasant place for them.

"Let's go on to the next item. There's still a lot of noise in the lunchroom, and some of the cafeteria people are upset about the messes that some teams leave. No faculty members have lunchroom duty, but the situation is getting awful. What can we do about that?"

Discussion Points

1. What are some of the primary issues involved in this case?

2. Is the principal being too demanding? Why or why not?

3. How can the principal identify problem areas, and once they are identified, what steps should he take?

4. How can the teams help with the problem-solving process?

༄ ༉

The Case of the Combative Leadership Team

Wide River Middle School's leadership team was large, partly because of the size of the school, which housed nearly a thousand students in grades six through eight. All team leaders were on the leadership team, as well as the counselors and the assistant principals; also included was one representative each from the physical education department, the exploratory team, the art and music team, the instructional assistant staff, the cafeteria staff, the bus drivers, the custodial staff, and the parents. The principal, Patricia Lord, headed this team of nearly twenty people. She had purposely made the leadership team representative of the entire school staff in order to gather commitment and support throughout the school.

This was Wide River's second year as a middle school, and it was also the second year for the leadership team. Previously, Wide River had been a traditional junior high school with a fully departmentalized organization. Ms. Lord had been assigned to Wide River after successfully reorganizing one of the worst elementary schools in the district. She had also been an assistant principal in the largest high school in the district, and she was known for her fair but caring manner of dealing with students. Last year, the leadership team had functioned fairly well, dealing with a wide variety of issues and policies, including some sensitive ones: dress for physical education, credit for make-up work, and discipline codes. In one case the team had successfully interceded on behalf of a pregnant eighth-grade student who needed help finding assistance and care. The team members had ended the year feeling that they were a united group of caring professionals who had significant input into the direction of their school.

This year's team consisted of nearly the same people, with the exception of the representatives from one of the teams, the parent group, the bus drivers, and the instructional assistant staff. These four newcomers seemed to fit in well as the year began.

The agenda for today's meeting had been distributed a few days in advance, so everyone knew what was to be discussed. Most members knew that one item on the agenda would cause some discussion: fund allocations. Last year the leadership team had been unable to agree on how the funds collected from the school's various after-school student activities, such as dances and parties, should be distributed. The fund was rather large, since each party or dance generally netted more than a thousand dollars. Ms. Lord had estimated that the upcoming Halloween party would net nearly twice the average, since the school was charging a little higher admission and had planned additional games. One possible use for the funds would be to help the teams buy supplies. The district had recently cut the teacher instructional budgets by 90 percent, leaving the teams with only enough to replace a few of the supplies they had used last year.

Last year, the leadership team had compromised by deciding to divide the funds equally among all the representative groups. The instructional teams were not pleased with this arrangement, especially since much of the money had been spent to reward good behavior on school buses and in the cafeteria. The custodians, bus drivers, and cafeteria workers had spent much of their allotment on pencils, candy, certificates, and, in some instances, toys and games that they distributed as rewards to the students.

Leadership team meetings were generally attended only by the team members. Today, however, several additional teachers and staff members had shown up. The first three agenda items went by quickly with little or no discussion.

"Before going on to the next item," said Ms. Lord, "I'd like to suggest trying a new way to manage the discussion that is bound to take place with this item. We are a big group, so to make sure everybody gets heard, I'd like to limit each person's comments to two minutes with no interruption. We'll go around the room, one by one, until everyone has had a chance to speak, and then I'll summarize the discussion. Then we'll open up the floor for discussion, but again limit each person to two minutes. I'd like to get out of here before tomorrow, folks, okay?" She looked around the room and seeing no hands raised, she began, "Okay, last year we took all the receipts from the dances and parties and distributed them evenly among all the representative groups in the building. What we need to do today is decide if we are going to use the same formula this year." There were audible mutters around the room as she finished. "We'll start with the eighth-grade Alligator Team. Tom?"

Tom Gately, the Alligator Team leader, stood and said, "I suggest we split the monies 75 percent for instructional teams and 25 percent for support staff, especially since we've had our budgets cut so sharply this year." He looked around the room as he continued. "We need the extra money for instructional supplies. I have no slides for my microscopes, no lab paper, no nothing. And it's the same for the rest of my team and for the other teams, too. I agree that the support staff needs some of the money, but let's not forget why we're here." He leaned forward, placing his hands on the table as he sat down.

"But if we didn't do what we did with the kids, you'd be spending all your time on discipline. . . . "

"Wait, George," Ms. Lord interrupted the speaker. "We're trying to let everyone talk, then we will discuss the items. It's Robyn's turn."

"Well," said Robyn Carter, the representative for the art and music team, "the music program is in pretty good shape, with the parent support and all, so I think we should go with Tom's idea."

"Wait a minute, Robyn, that's not what we said this morning," inter-rupted the young man sitting behind her, whose name was Bill McLaren. "If we don't get additional money, we won't have any programs or plays this year. We need sets, paint. . . . "

"Hold on, Bill, remember what we said about taking turns. . . . "

At that point several other voices were heard, and Ms. Lord tried to restore order with no success until she stood up and nearly yelled for order. As the room began to quiet down, one voice was heard to say, "You sort it out, you're the boss."

"Maybe," she replied, "but this team is the group that makes the deci-sions, and you probably wouldn't like the way I'd do it anyway. Let's try this one more time. Remember, one person at a time, people. Robyn, are you through? Good, then let's give Harriet a chance."

Harriet Schmidt was the team member representing the cafeteria workers, and she was highly respected. Two of her own children attended the school. "Well, let's think about what happened last year. Was that so bad? Lots of kids got nice rewards for behaving on the buses, and the cafe-teria has never looked so good. We had fewer problems than ever before. I think we should continue with what we did last year. It was fair." As Har-riet sat down, some voices were heard to disagree with her, mostly those of teachers who were all sitting in the same part of the room.

"Okay, people, please. . . . " The principal's voice seemed to get lost as the room came alive with anger.

Discussion Points

1. Why does the issue of fund allocation seem to be so important to the Wide River staff?

2. How could the principal have handled this issue differently? What alternatives were open to her?

3. How might the size of the group affect its decision-making ability?

The Case of the Overly Successful Project

Deerhorn Intermediate School was located in a small, working-class suburban area nearly twenty miles from a city. Long noted for its strong community connections and sense of independence, this school, which taught kindergarten through eighth grade, was envied by the rest of the large county school district. Parents were extremely supportive of the school and felt a sense of pride and ownership in its development and programs. The community was quite diverse, with about one-fourth of its residents white, and the remaining three-fourths a mix of African American, Hispanic, and Asian American citizens. Two major businesses, an auto parts assembly plant and a frozen food processing plant, employed the majority of Deerhorn's citizens. Both the plants had strong unions, and both management and the union leadership urged their employees to volunteer in the school. The auto parts assembly plant would allow employees paid time to volunteer in the school for up to three hours a week. The students at Deerhorn represented the demographic profile of the area.

The principal, George Weston, had been assigned to the school nearly ten years ago and had gradually established a faculty of dedicated, creative, and motivated teachers. A tall, broad-shouldered African American, Mr. Weston had a management style that might best be described as a "benevolent dictator." He was a very firm disciplinarian with the students, and his style with the faculty was such that he was always a bit feared, for he could be quick-tempered and liable to scold a teacher in the hall or in his or her classroom. Still, he was generally well liked by the staff, because he seemed to able to buffer them from many of the central office directives that plagued other schools. Unless a teacher brought about some sort of parental complaint or caused an obvious problem, Mr. Weston left the teachers alone. He often stated in faculty meetings that he did not like surprises or parent complaints. Most of the parents of the students liked him, since there were relatively few behavioral problems at the school and the thirty-year-old building was always clean, well maintained, and attractive.

The sixth, seventh, and eighth grades were organized into three interdisciplinary teams of four teachers each, a structure that Mr. Weston had established three years ago. No bells were rung at Deerhorn, but the three "middle school" grades adhered to a rather strict and traditional seven-period schoolday. There was little integration of subject matter, and the principal insisted that each teacher on the team hold closely to the district curriculum guidelines. The "advisory" program was a ten-minute period at the beginning of each day when the homeroom teachers took attendance and lunch counts, made announcements, organized the students, and periodically taught mini-lessons on study skills, decision making, and getting along with peers.

Two years ago, Mr. Weston had established a leadership team that he announced would be making many of the decisions that formerly had been his responsibility, including decisions regarding scheduling, curriculum, instruction, technology use and acquisition, and other areas directly related to the students. He would remain the primary decision maker in matters concerning the school building and major behavioral problems. The leadership team at the school consisted of one teacher from each grade level, one special education teacher, the counselor, the assistant principal, and one parent. All members of the leadership team were appointed by Mr. Weston, including the parent, who was also the outgoing president of the parent-teacher association.

During the first year of its existence, the leadership team had made several significant decisions about programs at Deerhorn. It had restructured the school schedule to alleviate a problem that had resulted from the school's need to share two school buses with the high school. It had worked with the cafeteria manager to eliminate some of the high-fat foods served to the students and to eliminate a sweetened fruit-flavored punch from the menu. It had made budget recommendations that allowed several science teachers to make large purchases that they previously had been unable to make. The team, though handpicked, seemed to be able to safely disagree with Mr. Weston, and in several instances decisions were made and changes implemented over his objections.

A serious problem arose when a new seventh-grade teacher, Myung Lee, implemented a thematic science and social studies unit about rainforests. Myung had transferred from another district school to be closer to her home and her husband's work at the frozen food plant. Her teammates were marginally supportive, yet admonished her not to stray too far from the established curriculum, lest she incur the wrath of the principal and the leadership team. Myung, however, felt that the unit would meet many of the science, math, and social studies goals of the curriculum. Further, she had taught the unit successfully for three years and was sure that it would again be successful. She had listed the goals at the beginning of her hundred-page unit plan book, and when she had presented the plan to Mr. Weston several weeks before, he had nodded his acceptance.

During the second week of the unit, one of the local television stations showed up unannounced with a camera crew to tape the students' projects. Although hesitant at first, Mr. Weston allowed the crew to tape a group of students working, and the principal himself was interviewed. The three-minute clip aired on the evening news, and as a result many parents and other community members called to ask if they could visit the school and see the unit and the students' work. The local newspaper, which was not often kind to the schools or the school district, also visited and wrote a very complimentary piece about Myung's unit. The district superintendent and three of the school board members visited her class and appeared to be pleased with the project.

During the third week of the unit, the leadership team was holding its regular meeting. One of the leadership team members, third-grade teacher Susan Smiley, rushed in just as the meeting was called to order. During the course of the meeting, she brought up the topic of Myung's unit. "I'd like to make a suggestion that we honor Myung Lee at the next faculty meeting. That rainforest unit she's doing is wonderful, and it has brought us a lot of free positive publicity. And why can't we have her give us a presentation on how she did all of that so we can try it, too?"

There was a deep silence around the room for several seconds before Susan spoke again, saying, "What's the matter? Is something wrong?"

"Well, Susan, not all of us are as pleased about Myung's so-called unit as you. We were talking about it before the meeting started," responded Tim Glatthorn, a fifth-grade teacher.

"Some of us are getting a little tired of it and, well, we aren't sure the kids are learning much from it," said another team member. "The kids are all over the building, they're noisy, and they must have a couple hundred books checked out of the library." Several others were whispering among themselves, and it was apparent that most of the teachers did not agree with Susan's appraisal of the unit.

"Have you seen it? My third-graders loved it! We're doing some writing about it now, and I'd like to do more of that kind of stuff," said Susan forcefully. Everyone in the room was now talking, and it was clear that the unit was a highly charged issue.

Mr. Weston interrupted the discussion by saying loudly, "I'm not sure that she is meeting the district curriculum goals, either, but the publicity hasn't hurt us." After a short silence he continued, "But you're the leadership team. If there is a problem with the unit, then it's your responsibility to correct it. I'll stand behind you all the way."

There was an even longer silence before Susan finally said with her voice shaking, "Oh, I get it. You guys are just jealous. She's getting all the credit, and she's new here. Don't you read the literature? The newest thing is curriculum integration, and as far as I know, we're not doing much of it. Didn't Dr. Foster, that consultant who gave the workshop, mention it when she was here last month?"

"I move that we ask her to discontinue the unit," Tim said. "Let's vote."

Discussion Points

1. There appear to be many issues at work in this case, both obvious and subtle. What are they?

2. How should the leadership team proceed? On what basis do you make that recommendation?

3. What aspects of the school and its climate could be used to help this situation?

4. Has the principal made any mistakes? If so, what are they?

References

Fullan, M. (1994). Teacher leadership: A failure to conceptualize. In D. R. Walling (Ed.), *Teachers as leaders: Perspectives on the professional development of teachers* (pp. 241–253). Bloomington, IN: Phi Delta Kappa Educational Foundation.

George, P., & Alexander, W. (1993). *The exemplary middle school.* Orlando, FL: Harcourt Brace Jovanovich.

Goodlad, J. (1994). *Educational renewal.* San Francisco: Jossey-Bass.

❧ 8 ❧

PARENTS AND THE COMMUNITY

The Case of the Old-Fashioned Community
The Case of the Flopped Parent Program
The Case of the Powerful Partnership

PARENTAL INVOLVEMENT IN public schools is said to peak at kindergarten and diminish from then on. Indeed, the level and type of parental involvement do seem to shrink as the age of the child increases. Yet, because middle school students are in the process of radical and pivotal changes in development, there is a strong need for parent involvement in middle school education. Kochan (1992) suggests that this engagement with parents must involve a significant shift in the traditional paradigm of parental involvement. Parents and the community must be seen as true partners in the education of children, and the partnership should involve not only such elements as improved communication, but also some kinds of responsibilities for school operations.

There is also a complementary need for other community resources, agencies, and businesses to have meaningful and productive relationships with middle schools. The authors of *Turning Points* (Carnegie Council on Adolescent Development, 1989) recommended that middle schools enter into partnerships with businesses, service organizations, and other community agencies. The partnerships would help schools include public service activities as part of the curriculum, help them engage students in meaningful volunteer work, and help agencies and schools provide closer access to services for students and families.

To be successful, such partnerships require additional levels of education, expertise, energy, time, and leadership on the part of educators. Parents and the community must be properly informed and educated about school affairs, especially since the educational milieu is fraught with acronyms, jargon, and poorly defined practices. Policies need to be clearly developed, written, reviewed, and approved so as to communicate the purposes and contexts of programs in easily understood and specific terms. Swap (1990) suggests that parent involvement programs should be founded on a three-part philosophical platform that includes clear expectations for school-to-home transitions, interactive learning that ensures student successes, and a statement of partnership for school success based on a consensus of beliefs and goals.

The interdisciplinary team structures and leadership teams found in middle schools provide a welcome springboard for such programs, especially if the teams work together synergistically to enter into strong parent and community partnerships. The time and expertise needed for effective programs can be shared and coordinated more easily in middle schools than in other settings where teachers operate in relative isolation from one another. Quigley (1995) suggests that any kind of volunteer or parental involvement program must also be clearly, adequately, and frequently assessed as to effectiveness and goal attainment. Too often, partnerships and parent programs are loosely structured around time constraints, field trips, and classroom parties and activities. If they are to be meaningful, parental involvement programs must reach far beyond these more elementary needs to include activities directly and cogently connected with the school's mission of learning.

Many challenges are associated with this significant and important aspect of middle school education, and the most important is straightforward, honest, and clear communication. As middle schools develop and begin the slow and difficult process of educational change, all stakeholders in the process must be fully and explicitly informed about not only the successes but also the problems and difficulties. Parents can often play important roles in the solution of problems, but they must be in a position of trust and be committed to the overall goals of the school.

The Case of the Old-Fashioned Community

"Cleveland Middle School parents, teachers, students, guests: Welcome!" The screech of the portable public address system followed Hank Ribbot's welcome across the gymnasium floor. "We're glad to have you here. And please note the new name—'middle' school—official as of last night's board meeting."

The group of about a hundred people settled down to listen as the principal continued, "Tonight we have a nice evening planned for you. And for those of you who came in late, there is child care in the domestic arts hallway, through the blue doorway to the left. The formal part of the agenda is pretty short, so there will be lots of time to visit your child's team area and meet with the teachers. First, I'd like to introduce Mr. Stanley Foster. He's the Grizzly Team leader, and he's going to talk for about five minutes about the team structure we've put in place. Stan?" There was scattered applause as Stanley Foster took the microphone and placed several overheads on the table.

For the next twenty minutes, three teachers and Mr. Ribbot gave an overview of what it meant to be a middle school. They had distributed a brochure that defined much of the terminology in detail, and they answered a few questions. After the presentations, the parents were guided to their respective team hallways and areas.

The school was a very old two-story building that had been restored over the summer into a source of pride for the city and the school district. The team areas were clearly marked with the team symbols and logos, and the teachers, parents, and students enjoyed a quiet but warm welcome to the middle school.

Mr. Ribbot had been assigned to the middle school last spring when the former principal of Cleveland retired. The new principal's only experience in middle schools was as a teacher, nearly twenty years ago. Since then he had remained in elementary schools as a teacher, counselor, and then principal. He wanted this assignment to be his last.

As the next three months went by, the teachers struggled to make sense of teams and an interdisciplinary curriculum. They mastered new methods and ideas, grew accustomed to having no bells, made new friends, got to know the students, and worked very hard. The principal was supportive and helpful, but he pushed very hard to get the structures of a real middle school in place.

The first signs of trouble came at the end of the first six-week grading period. First of all, there was a software problem in the new computerized report card system that would not allow the teachers to custom-design comments for the cards. As a result, most report cards went home without any comment at all or else bearing generic comments such as "good student," "good reader," or "good citizen." Second, and more serious, student grades were considerably lower than they had been in the past. For the next few days, Mr. Ribbot, the assistant principal, and the school counselor were besieged with calls from parents. Some parents of bright children were concerned that their students had not made the honor roll or had come home with Cs and Ds for the first time. One teacher failed one entire period of her seventh-grade language arts class. The principal immediately began making plans for an assessment and evaluation workshop for the teachers.

Parent complaints about other areas began almost immediately. Several parents complained that their children were not being challenged on their respective teams and wanted them moved to other teams. Other parents called to complain that their children's group grades in the cooperative learning activities were causing their grades to drop. Two parent volunteers, assigned to work in the media center, spent most of their time asking students about their teachers. The stress on the teachers was taking its toll as well; for the first time in years, Mr. Ribbot saw tears in the teachers' lounge. The good-natured competition between the eighth-grade teams grew nasty, and it included parents.

Finally, some parents organized themselves into a "school improvement committee" and requested a formal meeting with the principal and all his team leaders. During the meeting, the parent who appeared to be the leader, Ms. Johnson, repeatedly suggested that the community valued its traditional ways and took pride in being called "old-fashioned." She stopped short of threatening to go to the school board, but both she and the principal knew that the school board was already fully aware of the problems Cleveland Middle was having. Ms. Johnson was concerned that these new practices were shortchanging the students; from what she had seen, she said, their grades were lower and the students themselves were becoming more and more unruly.

After the parent group had gone, Mr. Ribbot sat at his desk thinking about their concerns and comments. Much of what they had said was true. The kids' grades were worse, and their behavior was not improving. Teacher morale was low, as indicated by a high rate of absenteeism. The principal's notes from his observations were stuffed in a folder, and as he looked over them, he tried to remember the lessons he had observed. Kids were listening, taking notes, doing worksheets, sometimes conducting experiments—not a whole lot different from traditional teaching. Teachers had neat rooms with posters, and signs hung in every imaginable spot. The halls were generally clean and as litter-free as a middle school can be. For the first time in a long time, he wasn't sure what to do.

Discussion Points

1. There appears to be a lot going on in this case behind the scenes. Identify some problematic aspects of changing to a middle school.

2. Do the parents in this case have a valid point to make? If so, what steps should be taken, and who should take them?

3. The open house at the first of the year is very typical. What other public relations activities should take place when a school embarks on such dramatic change?

The Case of the Flopped Parent Program

Bridgewater Middle School was located near a medium-sized suburb of a major midwestern city, and enrolled 725 students in the sixth, seventh, and eighth grades. Its constituency was about half middle-income families and one-third working poor, while the remainder were a group of upper-class, wealthy families that had been in the area the longest. As the community and suburb had grown, the cultural diversity had grown as well, and the present racial and ethnic mix was probably near the state average. The growth of the school had been slow enough for the district administration to anticipate needs, and for several years the school stood as an example of careful planning, cultural harmony, and effective learning. Its academic profile continued to be one of the highest in the district and the state, and the high school into which Bridgewater fed its students was pleased with the caliber of student it received.

Two years ago the school's principal, Josephine Coleman, and its counselor, Ralph McGrew, had been awarded a $2,500 grant from the district to
plan and implement an innovative family and parent involvement program
for the school. Parent involvement was one area with which the school historically had had difficulties. For example, less than 10 percent of the
school's parents usually attended an open house. And even though getting
members for the parent-teacher organization was relatively easy, there
were rarely more than five or six parents who regularly attended the meetings. Volunteers for such activities as dances and parties were always difficult to find, and even once identified, two or three would usually call to
cancel before an event. The one place where parents were fairly active was
the interscholastic athletic program. Bridgewater Middle sponsored a football team, boys' and girls' basketball teams, a girls' volleyball team, a boys'
baseball team, and a girls' softball team. There were plans to implement
track and field teams next year. Even in this area, however, parent attendance lagged behind the school's rivals. It was not uncommon for a visiting team to have more parents attend a game than Bridgewater had.

There were also relatively few parent complaints at Bridgewater. The
school's assistant principal, Mary Sue Weaver, dealt with nearly all the
behavior and discipline problems, and she received few complaints about
their resolution. The administrators had kept careful track of complaints of
all types, and for a school the size of Bridgewater, the number of complaints
was inconsequential and their handling had satisfied the parents. Yet the
principal, Ms. Coleman, knew that they could do better. She knew that if
there were more parent involvement in the school, her profiles would look
even better. She also knew that the school was bound to become even more
diverse as the population continued to change, and a good parental support system could help in dealing with increasing diversity.

The parent involvement program for which the grant had been
awarded included a series of parent workshops in middle school practices,
parenting skills, and early adolescent development. Each workshop was
led by groups of teachers together with Ms. Coleman and Mr. McGrew.
Several teachers also volunteered to help with child care for small children
in the school's domestic arts laboratory. Other teachers volunteered to play
games with the middle school students in the gym during the workshops.
The grant allowed the school to pay a small stipend to these volunteer
workers, to provide food and drinks for the participants, to pay for photocopies, and to send a double mailing to each home before each workshop.

Yet attendance at the workshops was very low. The average attendance
was about thirty, and those individuals represented only about twenty families, most of which were already involved with the PTA or the sports
teams. The evaluations completed by participants gave high marks to the
presenters and the information. The evaluation form for the final workshop
included a question regarding attendance, and the information provided

simply confirmed what Ms. Coleman and Mr. McGrew already knew: parents were overworked and tired, and would rather spend an evening at home than come to school for a meeting. After the final workshop, they also made a series of telephone calls to parents to inquire about attendance. Again, the calls simply reinforced what they already knew.

The district administration was now asking for a written evaluation of the grant award. The assistant superintendent was especially concerned about the reasons for the program's failure to attract more parents to the school. He had been hoping that the Bridgewater program would serve as a model for other schools. The final evaluation report was due in the office next week.

Ms. Coleman and Mr. McGrew sat in the latter's office discussing the program and what their report should include.

"Well, we can only say it so many ways and times, Jo—it didn't work, and it didn't work because the parents would rather be at home," the counselor said softly.

"And we might include the fact that we have so few real problems that parents think everything is just fine and they don't need to be involved," added the principal. "But that doesn't solve our problem, Ralph. We really do need more and better parent involvement here, but I have no idea how to get it."

"Should we include some ideas for another program in this report? But don't ask me for any. I am out of ideas. This grant paid for all of mine. Do you think they'll want their money back?"

"No, they won't want the money back. But they do deserve more insight than we're able to give them. In fact, I'd like a little insight myself!"

"Well, what should I write?" Mr. McGrew asked as he turned on his computer.

Discussion Points

1. The parent involvement program at Bridgewater seems like a good one. What is missing?

2. The information Bridgewater has obtained about the lack of parent involvement is worthwhile but also common to many middle schools. What other kinds of information might be helpful, and where might it be found?

3. The case does not mention other individuals who might have been involved in Bridgewater's parent involvement program. Who else might have information, and how should these people become involved?

4. Given the nature and characteristics of middle school students, what sorts of parent programs might be of interest?

≈ৡ ৡ≈

The Case of the Powerful Partnership

"**A**nd you will allow some of your employees, your technicians, to take off work to come here and teach computer skills? For the entire school day? For the whole school year? Mr. North, your offer is extremely generous, especially after you donated the computer lab to us last year." Bob Scott, the principal of McDonald Middle School, was sitting at his desk, looking in disbelief at the chief executive officer of North Industries, a local software development firm.

"That's correct, Bob. But the employees won't really be volunteers in the strictest sense of the word. They'll be on my clock, getting paid as if they were at work. That's a pretty good incentive, I think. And I know how difficult it has been for you to staff the lab. Your one parent volunteer is only here three days a week, and then only for a half-day. I know she's pretty good, but that's not enough. Now, I've developed a schedule based on your school hours and your basic eight-period schedule. See? We can have all three grades through a series of lab exercises by the end of the year. And next year, we'll build on what we've done this year. You know, the kids who are in sixth grade now will get something newer and better next year. I'm going to volunteer, myself." North sat back in the chair, looking pleased with himself. He was wearing khaki slacks and a sport shirt and tie. The dress code at North Industries was casual.

During the past year, North's firm had fully equipped a computer lab with sixteen personal computers, printers, cables, and software. North had even had an additional telephone line installed for an Internet hookup that was being used more and more each week. North had received only scant publicity for the generous donation, and had insisted on nothing more than a small plaque on the door stating that the equipment had been donated by his firm. The lab had been used, but not to the extent that the principal wished. His problem was staffing; he was already one teacher over his allocation, a necessity to make his flexible block schedule work. The district had allowed the additional teacher, but had refused to allow another, even with the donated computer lab. The lab had one volunteer, a parent, who came in three mornings a week; she loaded software, helped teachers with instruction, and taught keyboard skills and word processing to as many students as she could. However, the principal knew that this was a tremendous burden for this parent who had a challenging job of her own, and he also knew that she would not be able to carry such a load next year. The offer from North was a welcome surprise. Mr. Scott knew that the district was actively working to develop more partnerships with local businesses, and this one had the markings of a winner.

North got up, shook hands with the principal, and said, "Get whatever approvals you need, Bob. I'd like to get this started."

"Well, Mr. North, leave me a copy of the schedule, and I'll get to work on it right away."

Five weeks into the volunteer program, the principal became concerned. The first few weeks had gone smoothly, with the volunteer showing up on time to work with teachers and classes of students. The students were delighted that the new schedule allowed them more computer time. The problem arose when Mr. North arrived, unannounced, at the principal's office just after the last bus had left with its load of students. The conversation was cordial, but in the course of it North complained that there were several books in the school library that he felt were inappropriate for the students. He asked to check the books out so he could examine them at home.

The next afternoon, North was back in the principal's office. The door was closed, and the business executive had a serious, stern look on his face.

"Bob, I know how you feel about people trying to tell you your business. I feel the same way—I don't like people telling me how to do things either. But this time, I think you'll agree with me that there is a problem with these books. A big problem. But first, let me tell you how this came about. You know Grace Evans, your volunteer that I'm paying to help the kids? Well, one of the kids had this book in the lab, and the boys were giggling over it, so she looked at it. See this tab? I've marked the spot." He leaned over and pointed out the passage to the principal, who took the time to read it. The passage concerned masturbation. Mr. Scott knew the book and the author's work and felt that this author treated sensitive subjects very well. In fact, the principal, a former eighth-grade English teacher, had assigned some of this author's work as readings.

"Do you see? And these other books are the ones you told me I could check out of the library. Last night I read them. Bob, some of this stuff is absolutely filthy. Unchristian and filthy." North leaned forward and continued, "Now what do I need to do to get these and other books like them out of the library?"

"Well, I appreciate your concern, Mr. North," the principal responded. "And the district does have a procedure for requesting removal of library materials. Here's one of the forms you'll need to complete."

"I'm not filling out any forms, Bob. I just want *you* to go in there and take these books and put them someplace where no one will ever see them."

"Well, I can't do that, Mr. North. There is a committee that makes a recommendation to the superintendent, and then he makes a recommendation to the board of education, and they make the decision," Mr. Scott answered.

"You mean you're the principal, and you can't do something simple like take a book from the library?" North asked incredulously.

"That's right. And I agree with the policy."

"Well, those books had better be out of the library by the end of next week, Bob, or my computers will be out of your school. Good day, Bob." North rose from his chair, opened the office door, and walked out without looking back.

For a few moments, the principal just sat at his desk staring at nothing. He was angry and humiliated; he was also angry at himself for not seeing this coming.

Discussion Points

1. In this case, the principal and the school are in a difficult position. What are some of the key issues?

2. What should the principal's next step be?

3. Partnerships with businesses and community agencies are being touted as one way to help schools, especially if the partnerships involve more than simple donations of money and equipment. Yet issues of power and authority are bound to emerge. How can they be avoided or successfully dealt with?

References

Carnegie Council on Adolescent Development (1989). *Turning points: Preparing youth for the twenty-first century.* Washington, DC: Carnegie Council on Adolescent Development.

Kochan, F. K. (1992). A new paradigm of schooling: Connecting school, home, and community. In J. L. Irvin (Ed.), *Transforming middle level education* (pp. 63–71). Boston: Allyn & Bacon.

Quigley, D. M. (1995). *Building effective volunteer programs.* Harrisonburg, VA: James Madison University.

Swap, S. M. (1990). *Parent involvement and success for all children: What we know.* Boston: Institute for Responsive Education.

9

ATHLETICS

The Case of the Losing Team
The Case of the Crazed Football Community
The Case of the Chosen Cheerleaders

ATHLETICS AND SCHOOLING have been and continue to be inextricably linked in American education. It is during the middle school years that students, particularly boys, gain their first experience of interscholastic athletics. In the last two decades, girls' participation in interscholastic sports has grown with the rise of legal and legislative demands for equitable gender treatment in athletics. Communities often rally around their school teams, and fierce competitions and rivalries often exist among schools that house sixth-, seventh-, and eighth-grade students. In a 1988 study of middle school practices, more than three-fourths of all the reporting schools stated that they participate in both girls' and boys' interschool sports competitions (Alexander & McEwin, 1989). Pep rallies, booster clubs, and parent-managed sports support groups are common in middle schools throughout the country. Yet the subject of interscholastic sports remains a contentious one.

One look down the sideline of a middle school football game reveals the wide variance in size and physical development among middle school students. This disparity in development is one primary factor in many schools' decisions to eliminate interscholastic sports and replace them with intramural activities that focus on participation, teamwork, fun, and physical exercise, and place less emphasis on winning. Unlike intramurals, interscholastic sports generally have highly competitive selection for teams, a process that may have a significant negative impact on students' self-esteem. Some students never again attempt to make a team after being cut, regardless of their ability or talent. Gentry and Hayes (1991) recommend that no interscholastic sports be implemented before the eighth grade, and Romano and Georgiady (1994) strongly suggest that interscholastic sports are not appropriate for any middle school students. Romano and Georgiady (1994, p. 173) cite the incompatibility of developmental levels, resource allocation, and the fact that most of the activities are adult-oriented as sound reasons for the elimination of interscholastic sports at the middle school level.

Budget concerns are another factor in interscholastic sports. Athletic equipment is extremely expensive, and schools and parents must spend large amounts of money on uniforms, safety equipment, officials, transportation, training materials and equipment, field maintenance, and salaries. Disparities in school funding are obvious among competing sports teams, as poorer schools must often rely on donations and external fund-raising efforts to be able to supply safe and comparable equipment for their teams. These expenses can quickly overburden schools' already stretched financial capacities.

Interscholastic sports emphasize winning; communities, and indeed American culture overall, place much higher value on winning than on either playing well or participating fully. Parents can and often do put strong pressures on both coaches and players, and may also exert undue influence on school administrators with respect to athletic programs.

Yet interscholastic sports remain an important part of many middle school programs, and schools, school boards, administrators, and the surrounding communities are usually reluctant to eliminate them. Sporting events provide additional funds, though minimal, to the school; garner parental involvement and attendance at school events; gain coverage in community media; and, through banquets and award dinners, afford coaches and teachers opportunities to recognize some students who otherwise might have little chance for school honors. There also appears to be a positive connection between good athletic programs and academic achievement, student behavior and attendance, and parental support (Hovland, 1990).

The Case of the Losing Team

The night air was cold; the overhead lights lit the players' breath as the offensive team ran to the sidelines. The snap from center to the punter was too high and sailed over the kicker's head; he grabbed the football and tried to run forward but was immediately tackled by the opposing team.

"That's okay, guys. Defense, get in there. Get tough, guys, no scores," the coach, Dan Palmer, yelled as the Martin Middle School defensive team took the field. He looked up at the scoreboard, hoping it wouldn't say what he knew it said. The score was 58-0 and there were still six minutes left in the fourth quarter. He looked back at the players seated along the sidelines. Every player had been on the field—some, of course, longer than others—and all had had a chance to play. Dan was proud of that, and he was actually quite proud of the team. They had started with sixty kids of all sizes and shapes, and few of them had ever played any organized football. This rural area didn't have Pop Warner football, and the county recreation department sponsored only soccer and volleyball. Dan felt that the kids had learned a lot this year about the game and about being a team. And there had been no serious injuries this year. There was only one more game left in the season, a home game against another rural middle school in the next county. Martin had yet to score a touchdown or a field goal, and if they were to accomplish that this year, they'd have to do it next week.

"Hey, Coach, you happy with that score?" an adult voice came drifting toward Dan. He ignored the comment, as he usually did. He felt sure that most of the parents were happy with his coaching and his teaching, but there were always a few who seemed think that middle school football was second only to the Superbowl in world importance.

"What's your record now, Coach—0 and 100?" another voice came rolling down from the stands, this time closer. Dan kept his eyes on the game as his team continued to struggle. He glanced at his players on the bench; they had heard the shout, and they seemed to shrink into themselves as they looked down at the ground in front of them. For a moment, the boys looked like what they really were: twelve- and thirteen-year-old boys, little more than children, who felt strong and big and powerful when they donned pads, straps, and helmets.

The game ended with a score of 65-0. After shaking hands with the opposing players and their coach, Dan tried to gather his players into a group to give them the end-of-game pep talk that had become almost standard. At that moment, Richard Shaffer, the father of one of the players, tapped Dan on the shoulder and said, "Got a minute, Coach?"

"Later, Mr. Shaffer. I haven't talked to the boys yet."

"This won't take a minute, Mr. Palmer. I just want to let you know that several of us are going to try to have you replaced as coach. This has gone on long enough." Mr. Shaffer spoke in a businesslike manner. "Nothing personal, Dan, we know you have tried your best, and you like the kids and they like you, but we think someone else might be able to do better. Just wanted to let you know what we're doing." Dan could see several other fathers and mothers standing near the fence watching the conversation; they looked away quickly when they saw him looking at them.

"Well, Mr. Shaffer, Jimmy is a great kid, and some day he's going to be a good football player. And you can do whatever you like. So long." Dan walked over to the end zone where his team and his assistant coach waited.

The next day Dan was summoned to the principal's office. Mike Hart had done a good job of managing and leading the school. He was also one of Dan's closest friends.

"Danny boy, they're after your hide again." The principal didn't waste any time with greetings.

"I know. Shaffer talked to me after the game. I don't get it. He has never been a problem before, and Jimmy is a great kid. But, Mike, you know how I feel about football for these kids. You and I have talked about this lots of times before. I'm not going to back down. Everybody plays, win or lose—but I guess we mostly lose. What are you going to do?"

"Do you know who Shaffer is?" the principal asked.

"No, but he hasn't been around here very long, has he?" responded Dan.

"Well, he's been here ten years or so. He's the plant manager at the microprocessor plant. He's a real big shot, Dan, and he knows how to play the political games." The principal stood up and walked over to his bookcase.

"What do you mean, Mike? You sound worried."

"Well, the plant pays enough taxes to just about support the whole damned school district, and he has a lot of power." The principal paused before continuing. "They've told me to replace you, Dan. Dr. Powers called this morning." He turned and looked at Dan, who was now sitting in a chair, looking at the worn carpet.

Dan slid down in the chair, put his hands behind his head, and said, "Well, I guess next year will be a little easier, huh? I was thinking about quitting this coaching stuff anyway. It takes so much time it's not worth it. You know, I figured it out once—the money they pay me divided by the number of hours it takes works out to about fifty cents an hour. Screw 'em."

"They want you replaced now, Dan. As of today."

"What? There's only one more game! For God's sake, Mike, this is middle school ball! Got that? Middle school! Not the National Football League, not the Big Ten, but middle school! That's nuts!" Dan was standing now, waving his arms. "What are you going to do, Mike? Are you going to cave in on this?"

"I am this time, Dan. I don't have a choice."

"So what do I do? Just teach physical education? Is that it?" Dan sounded defeated as he walked to the door.

"Yeah. They're going to assign Tim Broker from the high school to take over as of today," the principal responded.

"Okay, okay. I can't believe this is happening, Mike. I know this town is crazy over football, but this is insane. I can't believe this. . . . " Dan's voice was lost as he walked out of the office.

Discussion Points

1. Athletics programs in middle schools are often the subject of controversy and debate, and this case is not as unusual as it may seem. What are some of the issues in this case that have to do with middle school students?

2. This case looks as if it will be resolved quickly. What do you think will happen next?

3. Predict what some of the reactions will be from students, teachers, and other parents.

4. What should a set of guidelines for middle school athletics include?

The Case of the Crazed Football Community

Buchanan Middle School was known for its successes, both academic and athletic. For many years, this 1,100-student school had dominated football, basketball, volleyball, track and field, baseball, and softball in the area. It was also recognized as one of the best academic middle schools in the state, winning many awards and attracting media attention. The teachers and administrators at Buchanan were recognized leaders and often gave presentations at regional and national conferences. The community of fifty thousand that supported Buchanan was proud of its middle school, and the school had never lacked community support. If the school needed something, someone usually provided it.

Buchanan's leadership team had recently taken a big step that all knew would raise controversy in the community. The principal, Beth Waters, supported the decision, but at the same time she wanted to make sure that the decision didn't erode any of her support. She had also spoken with the superintendent about the decision, and he supported it fully. Each board member had been contacted, and all had indicated support for the decision. The decision, though momentous, was simple: to eliminate football as an interscholastic sport and replace it with soccer.

The reasons behind the change were numerous and compelling. First, in each of the last three years, a student had suffered a major injury that threatened to ruin his chances for any athletic endeavors in the future. The bones of preadolescents are often still soft, and tendons and muscles are forming at rapid but uneven rates. Ms. Waters had contacted a professor at a major university who specialized in sports and sports injuries and found some astonishing statistics that supported the decision. The research clearly showed that football, even with proper equipment, has no place in middle schools. Furthermore, the substitution of soccer as an interscholastic sport held many promises: the high school had a strong soccer team, and the county supported a large soccer league for children beginning in kindergarten. The students at Buchanan who had been on soccer teams were generally physically fit and already had a sense of teamwork.

But the community had great pride in its football program. The rivalry among the high schools was fierce, as it was also among the middle schools. Parent groups and booster clubs formed central social points for many families in the area. Indeed, the booster clubs for football seemed to be able to raise funds more effectively than any other clubs in the area. Buchanan's football equipment was the best available, largely due to the booster club's financial support. Each of the various sports had its own booster club at each school, but the football clubs were the largest and most active. Ms. Waters knew that the decision was the right one, but she also knew that there would be some very angry parents.

Surprisingly, the school's football coach, Pat Miller, was in agreement with the decision. He was a very good coach and had been a college football star, but he had seen injuries too often, and the task of cutting boys from the squad was one that gave him a great deal of discomfort. He thought that soccer would be a good substitute. Because of the lower costs of running a soccer program, he knew he would be able to form several teams that could play against other schools that also had multiple squads. Thus, few, if any, students would have to be cut from the teams.

The announcement was made to the students during a full school assembly near the end of the school year. Although there was some heated discussion, the presentation to the students was done effectively, and the expected reaction, particularly from the sixth- and seventh-grade boys, did not take place. Instead, the coach was swamped with questions about the proposed soccer program. Ms. Waters, knowing that the decision would call for a public announcement, had scheduled herself to be placed on the board of education meeting agenda for the same evening.

The phones began ringing that afternoon. All three lines to the principal's office were constantly tied up. Most of the calls were from parents of football players or potential players. None of the calls was positive, and by four o'clock Ms. Waters was very tired of explaining the decision. She knew that the stack of pink message slips meant many more uncomfortable explanations still to be made.

The board meeting was very well attended, for a change. Ms. Water's explanation of the decision included information about the rationale, the research, the injuries, and the costs involved. She also spoke about the new soccer program, discussing which schools Buchanan would play, how many more students would be involved, and how much less expensive the program would be. There was no request for action on the item, so the president of the board thanked her and complimented her on the informative presentation.

As she was walking back to her chair in the audience, a man stood up and shouted, "You mean that's it? She can just dump football and there's no discussion? What's the matter with you people?" Several other people began shouting as he sat down, and the board president had to bang her gavel and call for order.

Discussion Points

1. What do you think the final outcome of this case will be? What would you prefer it to be?

2. What additional steps might the principal have taken before announcing the elimination of football?

3. What other middle school programs might be used to supplement the interscholastic sports programs?

4. Should other interscholastic sports also be eliminated? If so, which ones, and why? If not, why not?

The Case of the Chosen Cheerleaders

One might have thought the school had suffered a devastating tragedy. The small courtyard in front of the building held about sixty middle school girls, several parents, and several teachers. Nearly all the girls were crying, but some were visibly angry, standing with hands on hips or waving their arms and shouting. Two of the parents were hugging their daughters and also crying.

Near the front door of the school, two teachers were viewing the scene with obvious disgust.

"Were you a cheerleader, Sharon?" The taller of the two teachers asked the other.

"Yeah, in high school. I remember all this, Daisy, and not fondly. The ones who made the squad will be ostracized and become a clique, the others will be angry for weeks, and some of the most talented ones will never try out for anything again. Think of it—more than seventy-five girls tried out for three slots! And I'll bet I can name the three who made the squad." She turned to her friend and said softly, "Want to know how they get picked?"

"Isn't there a committee or something?" Daisy asked.

"No. There used to be one, but since Vicky Sheridan took over, she makes all the decisions and handles all the tryouts. Paul will get more calls about this than anything else this year."

"I saw all the signs for tryouts; they've been going on all week. I'm glad I teach sixth-graders—but I feel sorry for you seventh- and eighth-grade teachers. I'll bet it's been a zoo this week."

"Well, every chance these girls get they're practicing—in the halls, out front, at the bus stop, anywhere. And the nastiness has been awful. They get incredibly competitive and say terrible things about each other." Sharon turned toward a teary, red-eyed student who walked up to her.

"Ms. Jones, do you know where Ms. Sheridan is? My mom wants to talk to her," the student asked.

"No, honey, I don't. And I wouldn't expect her to be around much this afternoon. Have your mom call the principal if she needs to talk to someone."

The student thanked her, sniffed, and walked away. Daisy looked surprised but smiled as she said, "You're terrible! Paul is going to kill you!"

"No, he's been trying to get Sheridan off this for the last two years. She picks the students with the best figures and the most money, you know. And I'll bet there's not an African American or Asian American cheerleader picked this year, either—Angie made it last year, and she'll be in the eighth grade, so there is one black girl on the squad. And she wouldn't be there if Paul hadn't stepped in. I tell you, the lady thinks she's the coach of the Dallas Cowboy cheerleaders."

Indeed, the process of choosing the Madison Middle School cheerleaders had been a sore spot for the school's principal for years. And once the selection was over, Paul Vitaglio had to deal with the phone calls, the tears, the discipline problems, and the often cruel comments that kids could make. To make matters worse, Vicky Sheridan worked the kids extremely hard—too hard, he thought. There were Saturday practices as well as after-school practices, and the squad often traveled to competitions around the state that sometimes required overnight stays. Since the parents and booster club paid most of the girls' expenses and the board approved all the travel, there wasn't a lot the principal could do. Vicky provided extra academic help for the girls and often had tutoring sessions after the Saturday practices. She received very little pay for sponsoring the squad, and Mr. Vitaglio knew that she spent a lot of her own money on the girls. She probably spent more time at school and with the students than he did— certainly more time than most of the other teachers. Her classroom performance was very good, too; her language arts students often had work published, and they really seemed to like her classes. And the cheerleading squad was good, exceptionally so. The trophy case in the front foyer held more cheerleading trophies than awards for any other sport.

Discussion Points

1. Why should the principal be concerned about the cheerleading squad?
2. Teachers often spend a great deal of time and effort on this sort of activity. What alternatives might they have?
3. What steps can the principal take to solve the problem with the squad?

References

Alexander, W. M., & McEwin, K. (1989). *Schools in the middle: Status and progress.* Columbus, OH: National Middle School Association.

Gentry, D. L., & Hayes, R. L. (1991). Guidelines for athletic programs in the middle school. *Middle School Journal, 22* (3), 4–6.

Hovland, D. (1990). Middle level activities programs: Helping achieve academic success. *NASSP Bulletin, 74* (530), 15–18.

Romano, L. G., & Georgiady, N. P. (1994). *Building an effective middle school.* Madison, WI: Brown & Benchmark.

10

TWENTY-FIRST-CENTURY MIDDLE SCHOOL PROBLEMS

The Case of the Sexual Identity Crisis
The Case of the Multicultural Team
The Case of Gang Violence
The Case of the Immigrant Students

AS THE THIRD MILLENNIUM APPROACHES, Americans are afraid. Children are perhaps the most afraid of all. Violence abounds in the United States as helplessness and hopelessness drive adults and children to acts that reveal the callous cynicism of those who know that their own lives are likely to be short and violent. The media, particularly television and movies, often portray life's goal as the gathering of possessions, and moral and ethical acts as cowardly and ineffective. It comes as no surprise to most teachers that gang-related and other peer group bonding activities can easily replace family structures as students search for meaning and for ways to assuage fears about the future. Children need structure, and unfortunately they can often find meaningful structure in antisocial avenues. The twentieth century is ending with a darkening in the soul of the culture, and the culture is afraid.

Schools and school cultures are an accurate and unerring reflection of the society that surrounds them. There is little disagreement

109

that American culture has been and remains in the process of change. The United States, like other Western nations, is becoming more diverse as language and economic barriers diminish. Information has replaced industry as the main source of economic success, and the speed at which information moves is mind-boggling. At best, schools can acknowledge and act on these changes; at worst, they can ignore them.

Schools harbor all the challenges and problems that face American culture as a whole. Fortunately, school faculties and staffs consist of professional, caring, and highly motivated persons who entered this helping profession because they care about what happens to children. Teachers and school professionals are kind and generous people who also often find the world outside the school building frightening and violent. However, these professionals also bring to the school a wide and diverse range of perceptions, professional and personal experience, and opinions. The true measure of the strength of any school staff is deeply imbedded in these differences and the value placed upon them. An exemplary middle school staff—especially if arranged, organized, and led in a collegial and democratic fashion—will use the full extent of its diversity to solve problems. Martin Luther King, Jr., suggested that the nature of diversity binds the culture together in a unique manner. He said that "we are caught in an inescapable network of mutuality, tied in a single garment of destiny. Whatever affects one directly, affects all indirectly."

It is nonetheless difficult for teachers, like other Americans, to engage in acts that are selfless and participatory, or to act outside of self-interest. Teachers are human beings who are motivated by self-interest, especially when they are faced with the same fast-moving, baffling cultural environments and actions that fill the daily newscasts. It is even more difficult for children, especially those who are developmentally egocentric and unable to exercise higher degrees of abstract thinking, to perceive needs beyond self if they are subjected to a constant barrage of threats. In comprehensive studies of Japanese junior high schools, both Duke (1989) and George (1989) suggested that it is during the middle school years that children are most ready to learn about citizenship and group involvement. In most Japanese schools, nearly 20 percent of the school week is spent on activities that support group involvement, loyalty, and citizenship.

Middle school professionals must develop and build school cultures, classroom environments, and instructional activities that create a dynamic balance of safety, acceptance, tolerance, challenge, and democratic action based on the spirit of community and social conscience. The balance must also allow for healthy exploration and development of self, with appropriate ethical and moral constraints that support the spirit of community. The dynamic nature of this balance suggests that cultural changes and events can be addressed and used as springboards for discussion and citizenship development. Creating, maintaining, and reaching this balance is never easy and cannot be done in isolation from the community, but it is imperative that middle schools in particular make concerted, collective, and consistent attempts to achieve it.

The Case of the Sexual Identity Crisis

"**Y**ou said that I could come to you with a problem, Ms. Green, and I think I have one." The eighth-grade student stood before Jane Green's desk, towering over her as he did most of his classmates. Rick Smith was a gregarious, handsome, intelligent student who was popular with both students and teachers. He was the star basketball and baseball player in the school, and the high school coaches had already approached him and his parents about next year's athletic opportunities. Jane smiled at Rick and responded, "Ricky, I've known you since you were in the fifth grade. Have a seat—I'd be happy to talk with you. What's up?" She pointed to a chair next to her desk, and as he turned the chair around so he could rest his arms across its back, she continued, "How's your mother?"

Rick looked away toward the windows in the room before answering, "Well, that's kind of what I need to talk about." He hesitated again, and as he turned to look at Jane, she saw that his eyes were reddening and he looked very close to tears. She scooted her chair around the desk and put her hand on his shoulder as she realized that whatever was bothering this child, it was disturbing him deeply. "It's okay, Rick, you know that what you tell me won't go any further than the two of us—whatever is bothering you." Jane paused and immediately regretted her promise, realizing that the problem might be one that would require that she break the promise.

"Ms. Green, I think I'm gay." Rick's voice wavered and cracked.

"Oh, Ricky," Jane began, blushing. Unsure what to say, she stopped and took a deep breath before continuing. "Are you sure, Ricky? You're so young, and. . . . "

"I've known for a long time," interrupted Rick. "I came to you because Ronny said he heard you have a brother who's gay. Is that true?"

Jane was deeply surprised that one of her students could know that Jeff, her brother, was gay. Jeff lived in California, nearly a thousand miles away, and he rarely came to visit.

"Yes, Ricky, my brother is gay. I'm surprised that anyone here even knows that. He lives in California, and I hardly ever see him."

"How come?" Ricky asked.

Jane thought that the conversation was going in the wrong direction as she answered, "Well, he is very busy with his job, and our parents live near him. I can't afford to travel much, and he can't afford the time. We see each other during the holidays, though. We always go to our parents' house for Christmas." She paused, then asked, "Have you told your parents?"

Ricky slumped over the chair back, and said softly, "I think my Mom knows, but I haven't told her. I know she found some stuff in my room, but she hasn't said anything. I don't know, I kind of want to tell her, but I'm afraid she'll tell my Dad, and, well, he won't understand." His voice again began to shake, and Jane glimpsed tears in his eyes. The room was unusually quiet for a moment. "When did he, your brother, when did he know?"

"He was about your age, Ricky, and it was very difficult for him. And actually, it was our Dad who was most accepting. Our Mom had the most trouble with it." Jane remembered the evenings in the kitchen, her mother in tears, her father holding her and trying to console her. "That was a long time ago, and things weren't so, you know, open as they are now."

"Humph," grunted Rick. "They aren't very open now, either—at least in this town. You know what's funny? The only person who knows for sure, besides you, is Mr. Peterson—the guy who helps coach baseball. And he just came up to me one day and told me that if I ever had any problems dealing with being gay, to call him and he'd talk to me."

"Did you call him?" Jane was immediately wary as she recalled Peterson. He was a middle-aged former professional ballplayer who had retired early due to an injury, and he volunteered every season to help with the team. Jane recalled seeing him at school many times, and although she did not know him personally, he seemed to be well respected by teachers and students.

"No, but I almost did a couple of times. I came to you instead." Rick's voice was firmer now, and he was sitting up straighter in the chair.

"What do you need, Rick?" Jane asked.

"I don't know. I've read a whole bunch of stuff, and the more I read, the more confused I get. Some articles say you should come out and admit it, and others say to cool it. What did your brother do?"

"He hid it from everyone except his family. He even dated girls all through high school. But we knew. The secrecy took its toll, though, Ricky. He was very confused, and in college he tried to commit suicide." Jane was amazed that she was having this conversation with an eighth-grade student. "But things have turned out well for him. He's living with a partner now, and they've been together for a long time—fifteen years, I think."

"What about AIDS?" Rick asked.

"Thank God, neither one of them is HIV-positive," she responded softly. "But we worried about him for a long time. And remember, Rick, AIDS is a very serious concern for everyone these days, not just for gay people."

"Ms. Green, what should I do?"

Discussion Points

1. What advice should this teacher give to this student?

2. This situation may be atypical, since students generally do not know teachers as well as Rick seems to know Jane. In a more typical situation, to whom would the student turn?

3. What role should teachers play in helping students who are experiencing problems with emerging sexual identities?

4. What kinds of programs are available for teachers and students who are dealing with such problems?

The Case of the Multicultural Team

The seventh-grade Bulldog Team of Findley Middle School was about as diverse as a team could be. The hundred students came from socioeconomic backgrounds ranging from the wealthiest families in the community to the poorest. In addition, there was a growing population of immigrant and other minority students. There were ten Hispanic students, whose families came from Central and South America and Mexico, and eleven students from Russia and Southeast Asia. Of the remaining students on the team, about half were African American, and the rest, Caucasian.

The school district's response to the increasing diversity had been weak, but the board of education and the superintendent had made frequent public affirmations of their commitment to the minority students and families. Although Findley did not have a teacher for LEP (limited English proficiency), it did have a full-time ESL (English as a second language) teacher, Christy Jenkins, whose class load grew almost daily. She was an energetic, motivated teacher who had nearly twenty years of experience with middle school students; she spoke four languages and was now studying Russian at the local community college. Christy took students from their regular classrooms and worked with them in her room; the students liked her, and one of her more persistent problems was getting the students to go back to their regular classes. Her load, however, was tremendous and growing.

The Bulldog teaching team consisted of three veteran middle school teachers. They joked that between them they had more than fifty years of experience with middle school students. Susan Robinson taught science, and her classes were known for their interactive, hands-on activities. Indeed, it was a rare day when students used only a textbook in her class; she had collected large quantities of materials over the years and was very well organized. Students rarely misbehaved in Susan's class, because they knew the penalty was harsh—they would not be allowed to participate in the day's activities. Ray Briton taught social studies, and like Susan's, his classes were fun and full of active discussion and projects. Tracy Roper was the math teacher, and though her classes were less active, students still did well and enjoyed them. The three teachers shared a period of language arts, and this class was the team's one weak area. They shared the class because none of them liked teaching language or reading, and they had arranged their schedule so that, in Ray's words, "We'll all suffer a little."

This year the team was having difficulties, however, due to the diversity of the students. The language classes had become especially troublesome, because the range of reading and language skills was so wide. The teachers had little time to challenge the better students, few opportunities to take the needed time with the less advanced students, and they were spending inordinate amounts of time with the new students. Some of the new arrivals had no English at all, while a few, particularly those from Russia and Central America, knew only enough English to be able to converse with their friends. The difficulties spilled over into the other subjects as well. For example, many of Susan's science activities relied on written responses on worksheets or journals. Ray's reading assignments in social studies often came from trade books, and Ray was having a difficult time finding reading materials that had the appropriate information presented in simple enough language. He had altered most of his assignments and worksheets and was now trying to use three forms with different reading levels. The one area of success was math: Tracy found that numerical concepts were fairly universal, and although the students' calculation skills were low, she could communicate the concepts fairly easily.

Other problems were also emerging. Several times, students returning from Christy's room had been involved in fights with students from other teams. Three girls had been suspended two weeks ago after stealing makeup and cosmetics from another girl's locker. The students this year seemed to be forming more cliques and enforcing a kind of exclusivity in the small groups. Informal but strict dress codes seemed be present for some of these groups, and the students were particularly careful about wearing certain colors.

The Bulldog Team met three times a week, and during each meeting, the discussions centered more and more on student behavior, cultural differences, language problems, and the growing number of conflicts on the team. Today's meeting was no different.

"I had to break up another fight this morning," Ray said as he sat down at a student table. The team met in Susan's science room so they could use the large tables. "Sammy was about to go at it with some eighth-grader from Norma's team. I never did figure out what it was about. They were both speaking Spanish so fast I couldn't understand anything. He was okay by the time we got back here, so I didn't report anything."

"We're going to have to report everything that happens, Ray, if we're ever going to get any help," snapped Tracy. "The district is going to have to provide more ESL and LEP teachers, or we're going to start having riots. I'm serious, guys. I'm scared somebody is going to get hurt. I heard that some parents got into a fight in front of the school yesterday."

"Well, I saw that 'fight,' and it really wasn't much. But it worried me. It was between Sharon Piker's mother and one of the Hispanic moms. I don't know what it was about," Susan replied.

"No kidding? Ms. Piker? I'm surprised she got out of that fancy car of hers. She's such a snob, and Sharon is just like her," Ray said with a snide laugh.

"Well, this is going to be a rough year if this keeps up. And I'm sorry to disappoint you, but I don't think we're going to get help from anywhere. Our fearless leader in the front office spends more time catering to the few rich kids' parents we have left and ignores almost everyone else," Susan added bitterly.

"Thank God for the assistant principal. I don't know how she does it—being an assistant principal in this environment means dealing with behavior constantly. I'd go nuts," said Ray.

"You're already nuts, Ray," teased Tracy. "Susan may be right, but I'm still worried. What can we do as a team? I don't think that 'cultural fair' we had last year did much good at all. Besides, almost nobody showed up. And black history month just makes the other minorities angry. Besides, we need to do something now."

"What about the counselors? Can't they help us?" asked Ray.

"I doubt it. They have their hands full as it is. Maybe we should just regroup and get tough on these guys. You know, pull in the reins and tighten up. Maybe we aren't being mean enough," suggested Tracy.

"I don't know. Look at the Poodle Team. Those guys even walk their kids to the bathroom—and they have more problems than we do," responded Susan.

"Well, I know one thing," said Ray. "My language class is terrible. I couldn't even get started on my plans today. I spent most of the period trying to help Jose and Manuela; they're really trying, but with nobody at home to help, they're struggling. Are you having the same experience?"

"Yes!" said Susan and Tracy in unison.

"Let's stop and think for a minute," Ray said thoughtfully. "Where can we go for help?"

Discussion Points

1. This case illuminates a few of the issues surrounding school diversity. What are some other issues, and how are they related?

2. The situation on this team is becoming more and more common as the United States population becomes more diverse. Where can the team go for help?

3. If help is not available through normal channels, what steps might the team take to address some of the problems that are appearing?

4. How could the team get parents more involved with the team? Would this help with the problems associated with diversity?

5. The teachers on this team are also facing instructional problems and have made some alterations in their teaching strategies. What other changes could they make?

The Case of Gang Violence

Parker Middle School was situated near the interstate highway that ran directly through the city, and highway noise constantly sifted through the school. The area surrounding the school seemed to reflect the neighborhood; the concrete was cracked in many places, and the only place that did not have weeds growing up through the concrete was the basketball court.

Graffiti was evident on the walls and sidewalks. The school's chain-link fence stretched wearily from post to post, sagging and broken in numerous places.

Parker's interior was little better. The tile floors were worn, the hall walls needed paint, and wall lockers were sprung from their hinges. The door to the office, located just inside the front door, was propped open with a wooden straight-backed chair, and one pane of the glass office window had been replaced with plywood. The entrance to the building was framed by two metal detectors.

The school had once been the premier high school for the city district. It had been converted into a middle school in the early 1980s when the city built a new high school on the other side of the interstate. Peter Johnson had been the principal of Parker since 1987; a former high school principal and winning coach, he had cautiously implemented the district's mandate to change from a junior high school to a middle school over the past few years. Parker's twelve hundred students were assigned to three grade-level houses, and each house contained up to six teams. The interdisciplinary team arrangement had been slow to achieve success, and several of the teams remained committed to a traditional departmental format. Mr. Johnson had delayed beginning an advisory program, and instead continued to spend his minimal staff development funds primarily on sending staff members to state and regional conferences.

Officially, there were 57 different native languages spoken at Parker; Mr. Johnson knew that with the various dialects, that number could easily be more than 100. This part of the inner city had seen a tremendous increase in the number of immigrants, both legal and illegal. The growing level of violence in the area had driven many of the earlier minority cultures out of the area. As recently as 1975, Korean, African American, Vietnamese, Anglo, Hispanic, and several Middle Eastern cultures had existed together peacefully, but the area's growing poverty and crime had driven many of the small businesses owned by these residents into other areas of the city. Parker Middle School became a nearly perfect microcosm of the area. The violence, mistrust, and economic and racial problems of the area spilled into its halls.

Mr. Johnson, his three assistant principals, and the three counselors formed the core of the school's management. This leadership group was known to rule the school in an inflexible and punitive manner. Fights and inappropriate behavior were frequent and were dealt with severely and quickly. All fighting, regardless of cause, resulted in immediate suspension from school. Drug violations resulted in immediate expulsion. Pregnant girls were likewise suspended indefinitely. Until last year, these methods had proven fairly effective, and the school board had consistently supported the principal even in the face of strong parental objection to the methods.

This year, however, the methods did not seem to be working. Since the beginning of the school year, there had been three serious stabbing injuries and several other incidents in which police action had been necessary. At least six major gangs were operating in the school, each with its own insignia, hand signals, language, colors, and rules. There was also evidence that several other smaller gangs, including two female gangs, existed in the school. In all but one, membership was limited to a single cultural group. In response to a particularly vicious altercation after a basketball game, Parker's remaining games had been canceled.

The teams of teachers were forced to adhere to a set of rules that supported the administration's methods of control. No teacher was allowed in the building before 7:30 A.M. or after 4:00 P.M., and the building was closed, locked, and guarded during the weekends. Each teacher had an individual planning period, but there were no team planning times. No student was allowed in the library unaccompanied, and any student found in a hallway during class, without the appropriate pass, was suspended. Teachers were required to keep strict and accurate attendance records for each period, as well as to record any and all tardy students. Lesson plans for the next week were turned in to Mr. Johnson on Thursdays and returned by Monday morning. In spite of these restrictions, the teachers' attitude toward the principal was very positive, even though some thought his rules a bit oppressive. The teachers felt protected and safe, and, indeed, few teachers were ever involved in student unpleasantness at Parker.

On one Friday afternoon in the spring, two rival gangs, one African American and one Hispanic, met just outside the school grounds and fought a hand-to-hand battle, using knives and clubs. By the time the police arrived, three students had been critically injured, and more than twenty others had been hurt badly enough to require emergency room care. No guns were in evidence during the fight, but many of the school's students were openly talking about the possibilities of being shot or killed in the neighborhood.

Late Friday night, Mr. Johnson, his administrative team, three school board members, and the superintendent met to discuss their next steps.

Discussion Points

1. Violence can and does happen frequently, even in middle schools. What are some of the factors that contribute to the increasing violence in schools?

2. Discuss the principal's authoritarian style of leadership. What are its advantages and disadvantages?

3. What do you think the administrative team should do next? What options are available?

4. Some educators feel that strict adherence to rules and established consequences is necessary to maintain order in schools. How does this philosophy fit with what is known about middle school students?

The Case of the Immigrant Students

"**A**nd this is Tran Van Nhut, Ms. Miller. He's a new student, and I know he'll get along fine on this team," said Jon Villela, the assistant principal of Woodrow Wilson Middle School, introducing the slightly built seventh-grader to Joyce Schmidt, the Green Team leader. "He will be working with Ms. Lee, too. She'll give you his schedule. Good luck." Mrs. Lee was the ESL (English as a second language) teacher at Wilson, and Joyce knew that her schedule was already extremely tight and that she also worked at the high school.

The students were working in groups around the crowded room and quietly discussing the assignment. Several were out of their seats, leaning across tables and student desks, and some of the discussions seemed a bit heated. Joyce was in the second day of a unit about fairy tales and folk tales, and today's assignment was centered on discovering the common elements of such tales in various cultures. The blackboard had terms such as "magic," "princess," "evil men," and "handsome prince" written on it, and a Venn diagram was also displayed. Joyce's choice of this assignment had stemmed from the team's increasing difficulties with the number of immigrant students being placed in the school. She and the team had developed the small unit to help the Green Team's students better understand the various cultures present in the school.

The city school district was suffering from the pains of high growth, which was mainly due to an influx of immigrant workers who arrived in the city to work in its major industry, a large poultry-processing plant. Jobs were plentiful, and the pay was considerably higher than minimum wage, as much of the work was difficult and undesirable. But the plant was highly profitable and seemed insulated from recessionary trends; the demand for chicken and turkey products remained high. Many of those who settled in the city were legal immigrants, yet there remained a fairly large population of those who had entered the United States illegally. Two groups, Vietnamese and Mexicans, were predominant. Although the cultures and language of the two groups were quite dissimilar, the plant managers had successfully provided a supportive environment that welcomed and valued cultural differences. Only rarely did the three cultures, Anglo, Vietnamese, and Mexican, have significant problems.

The schools in the district, however, had not been as successful in accommodating the new arrivals. The district had limited resources for additional ESL or LEP (limited English proficiency) teachers, and there were extreme variations in the levels of first-language literacy among the immigrants. The classroom teachers were frustrated and overworked, and few of them had had any training in how to work with diverse populations. The school administrators, teachers, and counselors had all tried to convince immigrant parents to volunteer in the schools to help with translation and schoolwork, but with little success. School meant authority to many of these families, and the adults seemed to have a deep fear of schools and teachers.

Much of this ran through Joyce's mind as she introduced Nhut to the class. Her earlier experiences with Vietnamese children gave her some advantage, and she pronounced his name correctly. In addition, she knew that Tran was the family name, not the child's first name, so she introduced him as Nhut. Several of the Green Team students greeted the new student as she guided him to one of the tables. As they moved through the room, Nhut's fear and anxiety were nearly palpable; with her hand on his shoulder, Joyce could feel him tremble.

After last period, as she and her teammates discussed the day, Joyce shared her concern about Nhut and the growing number of students who understood little or no English. "I don't know what to do. I know I should be more sympathetic, but if we don't get some more help, I'm going to look for another job."

"Come on, Joyce, it's no different anywhere else," relied Tom Henderson, the team's science teacher. "And we've been luckier than most. We've had no fights to speak of, and I think all this cultural stuff we're doing is working. Did you know that Mike Boyer and Tom Smith spent the night over at Francisco's last weekend?"

"Yeah, I heard. But they all go to St. Paul's Church, and that helps," Joyce said. "What did you guys think of Nhut? Was there any problem with the name?"

"No, and he seems like a nice kid. It's funny, though, that none of the other Vietnamese kids seemed to want to get to know him. Did any of you notice that?" asked Debby Frazier, the math teacher.

"Well, now that you mention it, I did notice that," replied Tom. "He seemed really uncomfortable when I put him at a table with two other Vietnamese kids. Seemed kind of scared."

"I wonder what that's all about?" Joyce asked. "But it was his first day, and I don't think he knows any English at all. I'd be scared, too."

"Well, it's not going to improve, so let's try to think of some more ways to help the situation," suggested Tom. "I like these kids a lot, and I'm picking up a few words of the languages. I could even understand Miguel's mother the other day when she was fussing with him!"

Discussion Points

1. This team's situation is difficult, but the team members seem to be coping with the growing number of immigrant students. What are some of the reasons for their apparent ability to work with immigrant students?
2. What are some additional actions the team can take?
3. What could be some of the reasons for Nhut's apparent fear of the other Vietnamese students?

References

Duke, B. (1989). *The Japanese school.* New York: Praeger.

George, P. (1989). *The Japanese junior high school.* Columbus, OH: National Middle School Association.

GLOSSARY OF MIDDLE
SCHOOL TERMS

Advisor-Advisee Program   Regularly scheduled, small-group class periods used for discussion, teaching, problem solving, and other school or personal concerns. The number of advisory periods per week varies from school to school and ranges from once a week to once a day. The programs are based on the premise that each student should be well known by at least one adult. They are usually led by certified teachers and other professional staff members, such as counselors and administrators. Also called *teacher-based guidance, teacher advisory*, or *advisement*.

Block Schedule   Schedules that leave large blocks of time available for interdisciplinary teams of teachers to plan instructional times, schedules, and classroom activities. Blocks of time can be used flexibly based on the instructional needs of the team and the students.

Cooperative Learning   Two or more students working together on a learning activity. Successful cooperative learning places the responsibility for the completion of tasks on a small group of students who are mutually interdependent and individually accountable for the task.

Exploratory Programs   Regularly scheduled small courses, activities, and instructional activities designed to help middle school students discover, examine, or explore a range of topics, including careers, athletic and recreational activities, life skills, and other interests. Also called *mini-courses, mini-classes*, or *exploratory wheels*.

Heterogeneous Grouping   The practice of grouping students for instruction without considering achievement or ability, as opposed to *homogeneous grouping* (also called *tracking*), which is the practice of placing students in instructional groups on the basis of prior achievement and ability.

Interdisciplinary Team   A group of teachers from the different subject areas who are responsible for a specific group of students. Interdisciplinary teams plan instruction, schedule and place students in groups, coordinate activities, and are usually the primary contacts for parents. Interdisciplinary teams usually have a common planning time and use flexible blocks of time to schedule instructional activities.

Interdisciplinary Unit   An instructional unit, usually built around a central theme or discipline, that links the different subject areas into a cohesive, relevant, and meaningful whole. The length and breadth of interdisciplinary units of instruction vary with the topics, goals, or discipline. Planning interdisciplinary units requires extensive time, deep and relevant content knowledge, good team communication, knowledge of students' learning styles and abilities, and effective assessment procedures. Also called *thematic unit* or *integrated unit*.

Interscholastic Athletics   Sports programs designed to foster competition between schools and school districts. Teams usually consist of students chosen for their athletic abilities. Contrasted with *intramural program*.

Intramural Program   Athletic program designed and carried out in middle schools to facilitate participation and learning in a diverse range of activities. The programs purposefully downplay competition and emphasize participation regardless of athletic ability. They are held both during and after school hours.

Multiple Intelligences   Term coined by Harvard University researcher Howard Gardner to describe at least seven forms of intelligence that appear in all human beings and are used to solve problems, to create, and to learn. The seven forms of intelligence are verbal-linguistic, logical-mathematical, visual-spatial, bodily kinesthetic, musical-rhythmic, interpersonal, and intrapersonal. The concept is used in middle schools as a guide to planning instruction to enhance students' strong areas and develop the weaker ones.

Preadolescent   Referring to the period of human life between the ages of ten and fifteen that is characterized by dramatic and intermittent physical, intellectual, emotional, social, and moral changes. Also called *early adolescent, transescent,* or *emerging adolescent.*